TARNISHED VISION

Tarnished Vision

Crime and Conflict in
the Inner City

DAVID ROBINS

OXFORD UNIVERSITY PRESS

1992

Oxford University Press, Walton Street, Oxford OX2 6DP

Oxford New York Toronto
Delhi Bombay Calcutta Madras Karachi
Kuala Lumpur Singapore Hong Kong Tokyo
Nairobi Dar es Salaam Cape Town
Melbourne Auckland Madrid
and associated companies in
Berlin Ibadan

Oxford is a trade mark of Oxford University Press

Published in the United States
by Oxford University Press Inc., New York

British Library Cataloguing in Publication Data
data available

Library of Congress Cataloging in Publication Data
Robins, David.
Tarnished Vision: crime and conflict in the inner city / David Robins.
Includes bibliograpical references.
1. London (England)—Social conditions—Case studies. 2. Inner
cities—England—London—Case studies. 3. Crime—England—London—Case
studies. 4. Social service—England—London—Case studies.
I. Title.
HN398.L7R62 1992   307.3'362'094212—dc20   92–22144
ISBN 0–19–825751–1
ISBN 0–19 825816–X (pbk.)

Typeset by Pentacor PLC, High Wycombe, Bucks
Printed in Great Britain by
Biddles Ltd.
Guildford & Kings Lynn

For Anna

Preface

ALTHOUGH this study of crime and community action in the inner city is based on real events, and the experiences of real people, I have felt it necessary to change the names of those who feature in it. In most cases I have altered the names of housing estates, streets, pubs, clubs, cafés, churches, and so on as well. I have done this to protect both the people involved and their neighbourhood. Anonymity of place has to be ensured under the same rule of confidentiality as governs sensitive personal disclosures. If anything, it is even more important. If you are a tenant on a 'high-crime' estate, and you are perfectly honest, decent, and law-abiding, you may well feel personally invaded by yet another exposé of the place where you happen to live. It is not the job of researchers to compound the already considerable difficulties of people living in an area of poor reputation. Nor is it my intention to confirm derogatory stereotypes.

The place I have called the 'Borough' is an area where I have lived and worked, and established a network of personal contacts, knowledge, and information, particularly about local youth, over many years. I was brought up and went to school in this neighbourhood and the personal connection remains. From 1982 to 1986 I was employed as an instructor attached to a pioneering construction training workshop for unemployed youth and youth at risk of offending. The workshop was set up in the wake of the riots of the summer of 1981, as a voluntary initiative of trade-unionists, teachers, and youth workers concerned at the plight of unqualified and jobless school-leavers. It was jointly supported by the Manpower Services Commission (MSC, currently known as the Training Agency) and the local authority, along with a range of other initiatives, as what was known at the time as a Mode B Training Workshop, providing sheltered training for youth with special needs.

I was one of the early staff members of this scheme, and was a member of its management committee. From its inception the workshop achieved considerable success in attracting and retaining the interest of the area's disaffected male youth. In part this was due to its special ambience. An independent report once described the atmosphere there as 'informal but purposeful' and relations between staff and trainees were characterized by 'mutual respect.' In such a context research was possible, based not on observation of people from a distance, but on working with them to an end—the end being to improve their employment prospects. The advantage of what Lewis Yablonsky in his classic *The Violent Gang* (1962) calls 'live research' is that the researcher enjoys a comfortable strategic position *vis-à-vis* the young people. They had a basic understanding both of the role of the workshop and of my own role, which was to monitor their training, to provide counselling and support, and to help them get jobs. In addition, 'bad boys' who fell foul of the workshop's rules would be put under my direct supervision. To them I was not simply poking around in their lives for some vague research reason. (As Hammersley and Atkinson (1983) observe, for academic researchers the problem of access looms large.) The workshop's daily operations involved a continuing relationship with the people and conditions I am now describing. Of course, interviews with young offenders and their parents, meetings with community leaders, and discussions both formal and informal with staff from 'The Center' project, the 'Parade Club' for unemployed youth, and other local organizations were not designed with research purposes in mind. But, as Yablonsky observes, the essence and meaning of people's behaviour can come out more clearly in working contexts than through the administration of questionnaires and interview samples, however well designed. But the downside of such a research position is that, at the end of a day of being bombarded by exuberant and unruly teenagers, sometimes followed by evening meetings where people describe the area as being under siege, there is little time and energy left for reflection, or for collating and writing up data.

When I left the workshop I researched the locality further while working on a film for the BBC directed by Franco Rosso. A research fellowship provided me with the opportunity to conduct follow-up interviews with some of the young people I had got to know, and to write up further the troubled history of The Center community initiative which provides the narrative focus for this study.

Some of the material on which this book is based consists of notes of meetings and conversations with local youth and their parents, community workers, and residents' groups. Some interviews were tape recorded. Where no tape transcripts were available for quotation purposes, I have tried to reconstruct peoples' original utterances as faithfully as possible. In the Borough, a distinctive youth street dialect, or patois, has emerged which has been described as 'a kind of generalized West Indian English' containing numerous Jamaican and English working-class slang elements (Midgett 1975: 75). This patois can be used and understood by both black and white youth. Just as, since the 1960s, the styles of dress and music favoured by black youth have become absorbed into mainstream youth culture, so patois words such as 'wicked', 'crucial', and 'serious' have become incorporated into contemporary youth speech. This happened originally through the commercial success of reggae, rap, 'two-tone', and other forms of dance music. But in places of high ethnic mix such as the Borough distinctive ways of talking, or argot, continue to evolve which are learnt not only from the media but directly through interracial contacts on the streets. (For an intriguing socio-linguistic analysis of this process, see Hewitt 1986). For the benefit of readers I have compiled a glossary covering those street words, terms and phrases which occur in the course of this study.

This book is not, and does not attempt to be, for a range of reasons, an 'insider' account. However well I know, or think that I know, the people involved, and however much I may personally empathize with the persons and environment under study, I am a stranger in the social field. On one occasion I arranged to meet a former trainee from the workshop at a youth centre-cum-shebeen. He did not appear (a not uncommon occurrence), and I was aggressively questioned by some of the people in control of the place who did not appreciate the finer points of research into drugs and crime. Was I from the newspapers? Recently a woman photo-journalist and her companion attempted to cruise an inner-city estate in a car, taking photographs of the open drug-dealing that was taking place 'on the line'. She was intercepted by a group of people equipped with walkie-talkies. They took away her camera, threatening dire consequences if she did not co-operate. As one journalist put it, notebooks and cameras are the weapons of the enemy. On strange territory it is best to go with a guide who is an 'insider'. This probably applies whatever one's particular involvement, whether it be as a journalist, a film-maker, a detached youth worker, a sociologist, or an anthropologist.

If there is a guiding principle for doing research of this kind it is to be flexible. For example, an over-emphasis on crime and its consequences during meetings and interviews can often be counter-productive, producing misleading and unhelpful responses. The middle-class assumption that, say, a criminal conviction and subsequent imprisonment form a bench-mark in a person's life is not shared by everyone. One person's crime is another's legitimate survival tactic. Asking questions about criminal activities in unstructured settings is anyway fraught with problems. Above all, in soliciting information one has to be mindful of the social context, where, as one of my respondents once put it, 'the first law of the street is to lie'.

There is one side of the neighbourhood and its concerns that I was not able to reach. A fair proportion of tenants on the estate I have called the 'Satellite' are single parents. The prevalence of female-headed households and absent fathers is often regarded as a key factor in the socio-psychological development of children in poor communities. Yet, as a male researcher, nearly all of whose personal contacts in the area happened to be male, it was particularly difficult to gain access to the private discourse and concerns of women. My own experience has been that differences of race and class are far less of a barrier to research than gender. I am painfully aware that gender relations remain an unstated issue throughout this study.

D.R.

May 1992

Acknowledgements

GRAHAM ELLIS, the editor of BBC Radio 4's *Cause for Concern*, supplied me with material from his programme *Bouncers*. I have borrowed unashamedly from the insights and experience of Steve Dilks, Dave Howley, Sonia Plato, Will Conroy, Geoff Dench, Franco Rosso, Michael Young, Kate Gavron, and Matthew Owen. Professor Geoffrey Pearson kindly agreed to act as a critical springboard during the writing-up stage. I wish to acknowledge the crucial input of Hilary Walford, copy-editor at Oxford University Press. The research for this book was completed as part of a Football Trust Fellowship at the University of Oxford Centre for Criminological Research. I would like to take this opportunity to thank the Football Trust and its first Deputy Chairman Richard Faulkner for their support. Finally, I am especially grateful to Dr Roger Hood, the Director of the Centre for Criminological Research, for his support and encouragement of my work, and for his invaluable comments on the various drafts of the manuscript.

Contents

The youth are turning to crime
We'd like to ask our leaders
What do they have in mind?

popular song

1

Introduction

ONCE a group of young people had a vision—to transform their poor, divided community. But the vision was tarnished by harsh realities—violent feuds and factional strife, a chaotic local authority, ineffective and contentious community organizations, and youth involved in networks of criminality.

'Construction not destruction' was the unofficial motto of The Center, a community project which courageously tried to live up to its visionary promise. In the following chapters, a portrayal of patterns of crime among young adults is structured around the story of this and other neighbourhood organizations.

Some themes recur. Crime committed by juveniles and young adults is a key component in the 'tangle of pathologies', both individual and social, in the inner city. But juvenile crime is not accounted for entirely in terms of societal discrimination, familial deprivation, or a culture of poverty; nor is it fully explained by a lack of educational opportunity or of opportunities for employment training; and, as the development of The Center itself shows, it cannot be explained in terms of a lack of Government involvement.

Juvenile crime in the inner city has complex sociological and historical roots. One view is that among black youth it originated in the breakdown of the chains of cultural transmission between the 1950s generation of Caribbean immigrants and their sons. Societally organized control systems, in particular the police, became objects of intense anxiety, suspicion, and hatred among the new generation. The Christian Church is the sole institution of social control intrinsic to the culture that has survived the 'withdrawal' of the 1950s generation and its unintended legacy to the young of economic disadvantage. But it would be wrong to conclude that the people of the inner city lack a capacity for self-help. On the contrary, this is the story of intense efforts at local self-organization. But the problem of crime among the young is compounded by the variable

quality of the leadership that prevails in the numerous neighbourhood organizations. Some of these leaders prove out of touch
with the concerns of the young, others prove corruptible, or driven
by opportunistic, grandiose, and egotistical motives. In poor communities the leadership pool is diminished when people of talent and
ability move up and out. As one youth puts it later in this study:
'Sometimes when people in the community reach certain levels to
operate certain things, they change, that's it in a nutshell, they
change, all their thinking towards themselves, they don't really
wanna know the ghetto people no more.'

But the reason for poor leadership does not only lie within the
inner-city culture. It also arises out of the opportunistic and
manipulative ways that local and central Government supports
neighbourhood attempts at self-organization.

This book deals with the bad side of a neighbourhood. There
is another side to the picture. The area has also spawned
organizations which have been managed effectively and have served
the community well—for example, youth projects which offer
more than just a pretext for keeping kids off the streets. And,
although quite a few local youths do get heavily involved in crime,
many do not. Despite considerable disadvantages, some have
attained success in business, employment, and education.
Regrettably, these 'low-crime' individuals are seldom the objects of
research.

Many of the people portrayed in these pages are of African–
Caribbean descent. There is much truth in the frequently heard
complaint of community leaders, that black people are always
portrayed in a negative light, their very existence defined as a social
problem. In Britain there is a 'there you are, I told you, I worked
in the colonies, and I know what they are like' attitude, which
affirms that black people cannot be relied upon to conduct their
own affairs. An important hidden subtext to the story of this black-
run project's 'failure' is the private conviction shared by
many whites that it *should* fail. 'Those who talk about "all the help"
blacks have been given do not weigh in the scale all the hindrances,
covert and overt, reaching into every aspect of their lives' (Wills
1991: 15).

Nevertheless, emphasizing only the positive aspects of this neighbourhood, and highlighting the achievements and the joys of its ethnic groups and their organizations, would have meant overlooking one of its most pressing concerns, the destructive activities of criminal subcultures of juveniles and young adult males.

One half of all persons convicted each year in the United Kingdom are males aged between 15 and 21. The strongest predictors of known involvement in criminality are firstly sex, followed by age and class. There is a strong association between crime and being male, young, and from the inner city (Lea and Young 1984: 26).

High levels of crime within this group also produce high levels of victimization. In some inner-city areas, the most likely perpetrators and the most likely victims of street robberies will be young black males aged between 15 and 21 (ibid.). In addition, a distinctive feature of young black offenders is that many come from respectable law-abiding families. Some are academically able. There are young people going to jail who should be going to college.

The Chicago sociologist William Julius Wilson points out that social scientists have been reluctant to discuss what he calls 'inner city pathologies'. Wilson concludes:

It is not enough simply to recognize the need to relate many of the woes of truly disadvantaged blacks to the problems of societal organization; it is also important to describe the problems of the ghetto underclass candidly and openly so that they can be fully explained and appropriate policy programs can be devised. (W. J. Wilson 1987: 149)

Criminality among the youth of the inner city cannot be fully explained by the persistence of racist social attitudes and associated factors such as racist bias in the police and the criminal justice system, although these do create deep and serious difficulties. Even the destructive effect of youth unemployment, another real enough negative force, cannot explain everything. Lack of hope, living in a world of fallen dreams—this is a basic feature of people who are socially disadvantaged. Yet a recent highly acclaimed study of juvenile cocaine-dealers refers to 'unquenchable hope' (Williams 1989: 132), and psychoanalysis teaches that an anti-social act by a young person, such as stealing, may be an expression of hope (Winnicott 1956: 306). Such moments are described in this study, although admittedly, if you are the one that has been robbed or assaulted, it may be hard to see the hope that underlies your assailant's compulsions. Nor do I suggest that psychoanalysis is the solution to juvenile crime, although there are many individual offenders—angry boys, angry with their mothers, some of them described in this study—who urgently require some form of personal counselling or psychotherapy. Rather it is up to society, 'to meet and match the moment of hope' (ibid.: 309). The fact is that the incidence of persistent patterns of criminality is a measure of the extent of the failure of the community, its leaders, and its organizations to meet the hopes of young people. When hopes are wasted, and there is little sense of co-operation, people prey upon each other, and children are condemned to grow up in a social nightmare. As James Q. Wilson observes:

Predatory crime does not merely victimize individuals, it impedes, and in the extreme case, even prevents the formation and maintenance of community. By disrupting the delicate nexus of ties, formal and informal, by which we are linked with our neighbours, crime atomises society, and makes of its members mere individual calculators estimating their own advantage, especially their own chances for survival amidst their fellows. Common undertakings become difficult or impossible, except for those motivated by a shared desire for protection. (J. Q. Wilson 1975: 21).

How have the politicians responded to the challenge of giving people hope? Inner-city neighbourhoods were once supposed to be the natural constituency of the Labour Party. Some have been Labour strongholds since time immemorial. Yet, despite exhortations to fight racism, unemployment, and the poll tax, the Labour Party failed to inspire these communities. Throughout the 1980s such was the level of apathy and distrust of the Party that its already tenuous control of metropolitan local authorities was often left hanging in the balance after local elections. Even more hollow was the Conservative Party's glib rhetoric about the revitalization of the inner cities through the spread of the Enterprise Culture. After a decade of high profile, PR driven enterprise partnerships, private-sector initiatives, and the like, rising levels of crime, unemployment, and all the other indicators of acute social disadvantage remained. Indeed, during the 1980s such was the extent of the failure of the political parties to speak for the disadvantaged, that a prominent US community activist, Ted Watkins, declared, following a tour of the inner cities, that 'Any young black person coming to a leadership position in his community in England has got to be a revolutionary.' But what did these revolutionaries demand? What was their impact on Government policies?

After the widespread disturbances during the summer of 1981, there emerged from the inner cities angry young men and women, independent of the major political parties, who saw their mission to expose the injustices visited on their communities. One of them, who I shall call Lincoln Fredericks, declared forthrightly:

It's our time now. That's the reality. To get a piece. We don't want half the cake of England. We don't want half of the Parliament. We don't want half of the Government. What we want is a fair share of the cake. Stop taking the whole cake out and not giving us none. We want some. We are entitled to it. We have paid for it. We have sweat for it. We have bled for it. We have died for it. It's about time. And that's really where it starts.

The demands of this young leader were based not on a belief in socialism or liberal democracy, but on a belief in the special status of black and other minority people as victims. As Christopher Lasch has observed, the new leaders 'appeal not to the universal rights of citizenship but to a special experience of persecution, said to qualify their people to speak about injustice with special authority and to demand not merely their rights but reparation for past wrongs' (1985: 67).

The reaction of the political establishment to bellicose demands from oppressed and minority groups for reparation or special treatment is determined by guilt, by the need to win the ethnic vote, or increasingly, by the fear of disorder on the streets.

In many metropolitan boroughs during the 1980s all of these factors converged to ensure that local authorities accepted the status of black and other minority people as victims of injustice. A host of new Council-funded jobs were created to put matters right—from racism-awareness trainers, to housing-discrimination officers, and race-equality advisers in schools. This policy was based on the implicit assumption that the established systems of local government had been complicit in the oppression, or at any rate could not meet the needs, of minority people.

An unbeatable combination of windy rhetoric and haphazard service delivery ensured that in many cases this policy was of limited value to those it was supposed to be helping. In 1986, for example, the Labour Council in a London borough embarked on a policy, with Home Office backing, to combat educational under-achievement among minority schoolchildren. The intention was to provide in each school a teacher responsible for monitoring and advising on racial issues. The first appointees were dubbed by the tabloid Press, and by some teachers, as 'race spies', particularly when a primary school head teacher was hounded by the Council on the basis of unsubstantiated allegations of racist remarks. A Home Office monitoring report later stated that the scheme—with staffing costs of £3.2 million over four years, and annual running costs approaching £1 million—had been so badly organized that it was impossible to assess its value. The report also pointed out that the whole policy was based on assumptions rather than on any system-atic attempt to find out what minority pupils needed, for example by identifying areas of underachievement. The Council had not even ascertained the ethnic origins of the school population before embarking on the scheme.

Another central feature of the new politics of anti-racism was financial support for grass-roots community organizations which represented, or claimed to represent, victims of injustice, or which were owned and controlled by people from the minority com-munities. Yet, despite the subsequent proliferation of community organizations in inner-city neighbourhoods, it is hard to avoid the conclusion that these groups have done little to further the creation of a genuinely multicultural society of free and equal citizens in their localities, if that was their intention. One research study, which sought to assess the impact of community groups, concluded that 'The racial divide, so clear cut in the inner city, was not bridged by community groups' (Knight and Hayes 1981: 91). The report also concluded that 'Community groups did little to create a feeling of community . . . did not reach the poorest . . . are marginal to inner city communities and do not effectively tackle their problems' (ibid.). Also, 'the successes of community groups in affecting local authority policies were not increased by formal participation arrangements' (ibid. 90). In other words, community groups have had little lasting political impact. Indeed, in the eyes of the properly elected representatives of the people, community organizations are open to the charge of being unrepresentative, which they often are. This is partly because of the way in which those whose job it was to bring about change sought out and adopted local people as representatives.

The 1960s and the 1970s saw the enshrinement in community-work circles of the myth of the grass roots. In this mythology the real leaders of the people are seldom the officially recognized ones: elected councillors caught up in endless party political, and internecine party squabbles; local dignitaries, from the Larry the Lamb chained absurdity of the mayoral office, to the stereotypical do-gooder in the dog collar, and the bountiful matron in the flowered hat—all of these were viewed by many community activists as part of a massive institutionalized façade. Behind the façade they believed that there was to be found an echelon of uncorrupted and instinctively radical potential leaders who would never forget that their interests were the same as their neighbours', and whose great gift was that they lived alongside the people, shared their destiny, and spoke their language.

This was the myth that informed a great deal of what has gone on under the name of community action since the 1960s. The reality is that grass-roots community organizations have proved largely transitory or ineffective; in the worst cases they have ended up controlled by corruptible elements. One mechanism for this was the process of harassing government agencies to secure finance: randomly chosen, ultimately self-appointed, community leaders, who are answerable to no one, and who are well versed in the techniques of procurement of resources, provide negative role models for youth—and reinforce the view of those cynics among them who cannot see the point of becoming involved in public affairs unless it is out of self-interest. The goal of 'people power' recedes even further. This is the Catch 22 of community action. The plethora of largely opportunistic Government-backed community initiatives that sprang up in the inner cities following the riots of 1981, and the upsurge in levels of youth unemployment, may have actually reinforced this process. (The fact that the project which I call The Center, which came from the grass roots fostered by a community development worker, and was financially supported by the local authority, survived at all, despite a chequered history, makes it the exception that proves the rule.)

In the United States the conservative commentator Charles Murray (1984) has argued that policies that set out, in effect, to reward people for their disadvantaged position in society are pernicious because they change the system of penalties and rewards that governs human nature. Such policies, which reward people solely because they claim to represent and speak for the disadvantaged, are never the fault of the oppressed themselves, but the fault of the political establishment which, whether motivated by guilt or out of political necessity, chose so to reward them.

Murray's conclusion, that welfare systems are counter-productive because they create and promote a dependency culture among the poor, may be welcome news to the prosperous, who can then sit back and enjoy their tax cuts untrammelled by guilt. Equally, exposés of the anti-racist antics of leftist councils, and of the corruption and incompetence of grass-roots organizations which claim to represent the disadvantaged, can have a similarly consoling effect. Norman Mailer believes that Tom Wolfe's best-selling novel *The Bonfire of the Vanities*, which portrays charlatan ghetto leaders Mau-Mauing the Flak Catchers of New York City, owed part of its enormous success to the reassurance it offered the rich: 'You may be bad,' Wolfe was saying in effect, 'but, brother, the people down at the bottom are unspeakably worse' (Mailer 1991: 124).

Excoriating the victims may make the privileged feel better. But it does not explain the inadequacy of the inner-city response to injustice. It should not be forgotten that grass-roots community leaders, whatever their demands and whatever their personal qualities, face challenges from at least three directions at once: first, from the people of the area whose interests they are supposed to re-present; secondly, from the Government funding agencies to whom they must turn for material support; and, if things do not improve in the area and agreed objectives are not met, from discontented co-workers. Above all, it is invariably the financial support from Government on which the physical survival of these Government fighters depends. Many are in the position of Barabas, the hero of

Christopher Marlowe's *The Jew of Malta*, endlessly wheeler-dealing but essentially trapped, a helpless victim of the machinations of warring factions.

> And thus far roundly goes the business:
> Thus loving neither, will I live with both,
> Making a profit on my policy;
> And he from whom my most advantage comes,
> Shall be my friend.
> This is the life, we Jews are used to lead;
> And reason too, for Christians do the like.
>
> Act 5, ll.2212–18

This is the political predicament of inner-city leaders, 'Ensnared in the confusion of competing strategies, muddled identities and contentious efforts at organisation and leadership' (Dench 1986: 131).

Finally, the scale of local problems faced by community organizations in the inner cities cannot be overestimated. In the 'other England' of unemployment and poverty, a youth leader tells how 'the boys hate the police because they stand between them and what they want—money', a teacher reports that an 8-year-old pupil keeps breaking into school and killing all the fish in the fishpond, a young man of 17 (a former trainee of mine) dies following an argument over whether a pair of 'crocs' he was wearing were genuine animal skin, and every week the local Press records stomach-turning incidents of what Paul Harrison calls, 'the tortuous depravity that lurks in the darker corners of the inner city' (1988: 325). The ethic of self-preservation, of 'dog eat dog', is not only reflected in rising crime rates. It is also reflected in the conviction that envy and exploitation must dominate even the most intimate relations.

> Man to man is so unjust
> You don't know who to trust
> Your worse enemy could be your best friend
> Your best friend, your worst enemy.
>
> Bob Marley

Crime in the inner city is related to complex socio-psychological factors concerning young offenders' attitudes towards their elders and their peers, their individual motives, their dreams and hopes, the personal choices they make, and the roles they prefer to adopt in the dramas of their locality. The story told here is but one more act in the theatre of survival that is performed daily in the inner cities of the United Kingdom.

In party political circles, the concept of empowerment is in vogue. A bureaucratic variant on the myth of grass-roots people power referred to earlier, empowerment is based on a middle-class Consumers' Association model of a judicious and discerning citizenry making rational choices and coming to informed decisions about public affairs. In the 'other England', talk of empowerment, and of self-organization at the grass roots, can sound blithely optimistic. Nevertheless, this whole debate does show that it is increasingly recognized that positive social transformation cannot be achieved by governmental programmes alone. How to produce hopeful solutions from within the cultures of the disadvantaged? The question of who takes on the leadership after the uprising needs to be answered. Jesse Jackson once urged committee leaders in England not to lose hope. 'If you run, you may lose. But if you don't run, you are guaranteed to lose,' he said. For, as Richard McGahey has asserted, 'It is difficult, if not impossible, to imagine substantial reductions in crime and social dislocation among the urban poor without leadership and assistance from the minority community itself' (1987: 265).

2
Prologue

IN the shadow of the gaunt tower blocks of the Satellite Estate, Wayne Robinson, 23, stamps up and down the Parade, the estate's dilapidated shopping precinct. Sometimes he stops abruptly midstride and shakes a fist at the steel-mesh shutters of a disused shopfront which once housed the Lee Ho Fung Chinese Takeaway. Then he carries on marching rigidly up and down the precinct, as passersby swerve to avoid him. One evening a few years previously an elderly Chinese man who once worked at the takeaway was beaten to death while waiting for a lift to take him to his flat in one of the tower blocks on the Estate. Wayne Robinson, unemployed, with a history of acute disordered behaviour, had been sighted in the vicinity. He was visited by the police at home, and then taken to the Police Station, where he was closely interrogated about this 'mugging that went wrong'. Following this his distraught mother, a district nurse, disowned him. The murder aroused strong feelings in the locality. The victim had been well liked and this appeared to be a particularly senseless and cowardly act. Prominent in the chorus of indignation against Wayne Robinson was Roy Marshall, who was described by his former headmaster as 'an intelligent and serious-minded young man'. Roy's father, a civil servant, was a leading figure in the locality, prominent in community campaigns, in which capacity his belligerent negotiating style had earned him the nickname Mr T.

To the surprise of the neighbourhood, 'Mr T's boy' was one of those who was eventually charged with the murder. At the trial it emerged that the elderly victim had been repeatedly kicked about the face and head, and a few pounds in cash had been stolen from him. A witness recognized the culprits as people with whom he had played cricket at school. At the end of the trial 'Mr T's boy' was sentenced to life imprisonment. His shattered father took sick leave from his job, followed by early retirement. Years later residents recalled to a visiting reporter 'that Chinaman who got killed. That was a shame, he was a nice man,' and they still speak with anger of his killer's duplicity, and the shame and disgrace that he brought on his family. But in the endless pressure of the inner city, where the most important thing is to survive, no one can ever be certain of people's true motivations. 'Mr T's boy' was egotistical, defensive. How real was the role he chose to play before his peers? Some writing scratched on a wall reads:

> You never know
> What is really going down
> In Chinatown

Meanwhile Wayne Robinson continues his lonely vigil.

A short distance from the Parade, up the noisy arterial road, with its never-ending stream of heavy goods vehicles heading north, stands the gleaming new glass and pressed-steel construction of The Center, a large and ambitious community initiative, which took six years to complete at an estimated cost of £6 million.

The Center was built to provide solutions to the neighbourhood's problems, and so help reduce the incidence of predatory crime. Yet for long periods The Center was eerily empty. Scarcely used by the local community, underfunded, its impact on crime and unemployment was minimal. There were times when this project, envisaged as a symbol of hope, became a source of confrontation in the community it was intended to serve.

The seemingly intractable problems associated with neighbourhoods of high crime and high unemployment; the fight for social and economic advancement by some sections of the community, and the scarcely fathomable destructive motivations of others; the inner city as a battleground of political ideologies—these form the background to the story of the rise of The Center.

3

The Borough

THE Borough—motto 'Stand Together'—has one of the highest proportions of people from ethnic minorities in the United Kingdom and the European Community. It was formed in the 1960s, following the 1963 Local Government Act which merged many old boroughs. In the poor south of the Borough over half the population is black or Asian, and unemployment during the 1980s was well above the national average. Much of South Borough consists of a ribbon of austere, remote-looking multi-high-rise estates, which a local punk poet once dubbed Satellite City, because 'they might as well be on another planet.' Unemployment on these estates has been estimated to have been about twice as high as in surrounding areas. Social geographers have pointed out the paradox that these estates are all within reasonable travelling distance of other, more prosperous, areas of the city where there are low rates of unemployment and lots of job vacancies. 'The paradox exists of high rates of unemployment and of vacant jobs side by side,' but 'the jobs are skilled ones needing education and training which the unemployed conspicuously lack' (Hall 1981: 45). Consequently these estates have become market grounds for 'the uncharted operations of the informal economy' (ibid.). All of them are designated high-crime areas by the police. Burglaries, street robberies, and the sale of drugs and stolen goods are a common source of income for youths in these neighbourhoods, and legitimate employment options, in particular for unskilled and poorly educated young black men, remain scarce.

In practice, however, such heavy pockets of crime and unemployment are not quite so easily distinguishable. Some fifty thousand people live in the few square miles that comprise South Borough. The area ranks as one of the most densely populated in the world.

It is an ugly suburban sprawl. Clumps of forbidding tower blocks and huge grey-brick gas holders punctuate the skyline. The landscape is intersected by deep escarpments containing rivers of railway, overhung with ponderous iron footbridges. Residential areas are intersected at random by motorways and trunk roads and a convoluted, permanently congested, local traffic system. Pockets of owner-occupied Edwardian terraced and 1930s semi-detached housing coexist in close proximity to heavy goods vehicle parks, builders' yards, and storage depots.

At weekends the local roads and motorway system are clogged with saloon cars carrying consumer-minded families from all over the city. They are heading for the area's massive drive-in shopping centres, replete with parking facilities spreading over several acres. Some of the largest household names in DIY, domestic furnishings, and food-retailing chains in Europe have megastores here. Together they constitute a major new source of employment for local youth.

In the residential parts of the area there is little open space, apart from a few neat, postage-stamp-sized parks, such as Jubilee Park, filled with ornamental rock gardens and bandstands, and girded by ornate black Victorian railings. Other legacies from the age of municipal socialism include scout halls, the general hospital, and several old Church of England and Catholic schools. These schools are grim, institutional buildings—long echoing corridors, winding stone staircases, tiled walls. They were built to withstand the onslaughts of generations of unwilling young inmates, and they have succeeded. Since the introduction of Comprehensive secondary schools in the 1960s, attempts have been made to refurbish these forbidding environments, to dispel forever the associations of school drill and exercise yard. However, in one school, the latest line in local-education-authority fixtures and fittings and a bright new entrance sign are not enough. A side entrance is still guarded by the faded insignia of an earlier morality—BOYS/GIRLS.

In the middle of what remains of the old town centre in South Borough stands another relic of the area's past—the Victory Monument, an ornate high-Victorian symbol of civic and national pride. Permanently hemmed in by swirling lanes of sluggish driver-only double-decker buses, its plinth is covered in graffiti announcing the coming of the Big Youth Posse.

For nearly a century an unremarkable red-bricked building just off the old High Road has served as the Police Station. Outside, the old blue lamp, upholder of the Victorian proprieties, burns day and night. But inside things have changed. The overwhelming impression is that the station is staffed by white men and that black people are almost exclusively detainees (see NACRO 1991). From Dixon of Dock Green to a taste of South Africa.

Very few black or Asian people are seen in positions of authority in the Police Station. Yet the population of South Borough is very ethnically diverse. There are substantial communities of Pakistanis, Bengalis, Indians, Kenya and Uganda Asians, Caribbeans, Irish, and Africans. A transient population of gypsies, travellers, and homeless young people, mainly new arrivals from southern Ireland, live rough or in squatted houses. But this is no exciting cultural melting-pot. It is as though a cosmopolitan milieu cannot flourish in the stifling anonymity of its suburban setting.

Although South Borough is ethnically complex, it is homogeneous in terms of class. It is overwhelmingly lower-middle and working class. At one time the imposing four-and five-storey houses that flank the old town centre would all have boasted complements of live-in domestic servants. Now it is hard to imagine the process of gentrification, whereby middle-class professionals reclaim such handsome old properties from the indigenous population, ever making its mark here.

After the war, new suburbs and overspills sprang up in the green belt around the city, and many people moved from South Borough to better themselves. This created a surplus of older housing in the area. Some properties were barely maintained at all and became ripe for compulsory purchase and subsequent demolition. Many old properties were utilized as, or converted into, lodging-houses. The area quickly became known as 'bed-sit land', a grim, grey twilight zone for transients, migrant workers, and the unattached. Typical of the 'lodgers' was the southern Irish man who crossed the Irish Sea to take advantage of the building boom of the 1960s. Fresh from the overcrowded ferry boats, he faced 'the discomfort of shabby "digs" which provide a bed at night and nothing more, long hours, loneliness and frustration—these are the initial realities of his new life in Britain' (J. A. Jackson 1963: 71).

The presence of an Irish labouring class, with a reputation for drinking and fighting, encouraged the popular perception of the area as a rough and dangerous place. As one social historian observed, 'From early in the eighteenth century the Irish in Britain appear to have been, to some extent, associated with the problem of crime' (ibid.: 57). During the 1950s attempts were made to find a causal connection between Irish immigration and the rising numbers of cases of robbery with violence. 'The Irish are a young population, with many single men working in predominantly unskilled occupations. These are the characteristics of the majority of offenders in cases of robbery with violence who are generally aged between 17 and 30, are single, and in the case of more than half of them, are labourers, (ibid.: 67). Irish men were more commonly associated, however, with another kind of 'crime': riot and affray, drunk and disorderly, the crime of disorder. The Saturday night drunken brawl, and other rituals of pent-up fear and frustration, were reputedly regularly played out on the Old High Road of South Borough at closing time.

The post-war decades also saw the arrival of another settler population, this time from the Caribbean. Like the majority of newcomers, they chose the area not for its scenery, but for the cheap lodgings and rented houses, and for the lack of 'no-coloureds' signs.

The new settlers were a markedly religious, respectable, and law-abiding community. But limited skills and lack of opportunity for education and training meant that they were forced to take up dirty, unskilled, poorly paid, and inconvenient jobs which had been abandoned by white workers. But, despite this, they were sustained by the hope of a better life for their children. As John Pitts has written:

They had hoped that their children, like the children of previous waves of immigrants to the United Kingdom, would achieve material success and enhanced social status. Their teachers in the Caribbean had assured them that in the land of the mother of Parliaments, and the fairest police force in the world, every citizen would be equal before the law, be free to succeed. Instead the experience has been one of downward social mobility, material failure and eventual ghettoisation'. (1988: 132)

Many of the men sheltered under the conviction that their stay in England was only temporary and that one day they would return to their real home.

Until the onset of the 1970s the area remained predominantly Irish in character. *Once a Catholic*, Mary O'Malley's play about an Irish convent girl growing up in the 1950s, was set in a place like this. Today, despite the fact that it is outnumbered by Asian and African–Caribbean people, the Irish community still retains a strong presence. For example, a number of building contractors are concentrated in the area, and there is a proliferation of builders' yards, timber yards, and builders' supply merchants. DAVE O'HARA, HARRY RYAN, S. MURPHY, L. FITZGERALD—the names on the builders' boards confirm the Irish domination of the building trade. In contrast, and despite the fact that the construction industry—in particularly carpentry and joinery—is the most popular career preference among black school-leavers, there is scarcely a single major African–Caribbean employer among the bigger subcontractors.

The management of leisure and entertainment, such as bars and betting shops, also reflects the Irish historical connection, as opposed to the strong numerical black presence. The majority of publicans and bar-workers, and betting-shop managers, are of Irish descent. Few are of Caribbean origin.

Much of the work-force in South Borough is employed in the retailing and services sector. Industrially, the area has traditionally been dominated by light engineering, manufacturing centred on industrial and trading estates, and Business Parks. Numerous light industrial concerns and small-scale manufacturers come and go in the neighbourhood as the economy peaks and troughs.

The area has its own traditions of steadfast trade unionism. In the 1930s it was known in the Labour movement as the Red Borough. It had a strong and active Trades Council. Trade-union organization reflected the ethnic composition of the work-force. A number of convenors and shop stewards were West Indian, Asian, or Irish. During the 1970s a protracted, and often violent, struggle for the right of workers to belong to a trade union was fought out on the run-down residential back streets. The Chair of the Trades Council stated that the Borough, with its leftist traditions, 'was a bloody good place for the strike to happen'.

The strikers drew thousands of supporters from among trade-unionists throughout the country. Police tactics to contain the mass pickets took on the character of a military operation. The local character of the dispute was forgotten. The people who had taken industrial action were not the skilled, white, male, organized working-class stereotypes traditionally in the forefront of industrial disputes. They were far more indigenous to the area. The work-force of many of the small companies in the neighbourhood was mainly Asian, with a majority of Gujerati women. Many came from families who had settled in the area as penniless refugees from East Africa, for whom a second income earned on a factory assembly line was desperately needed. The strike had been lead by an Asian woman worker (see A. Wilson 1978: 67).

Since that dispute, in the high streets and on the corners of the shabby rows of shops that intersperse the residential enclaves, people from the Asian community have gradually emerged as the dominant business and commercial presence. This mainly takes the form of family-owned strings of newsagents and grocery stores, but also electrical and DIY stores and a plethora of other retail outlets. The Asian-owned businesses are often both family owned and family run, and tend to employ very few whites, or people of African–Caribbean descent. The scattering of black-owned business interests is concentrated around hairdressing, record and clothing stores, a taxi service, a butcher's shop, restaurants and cafés, and a few newsagents.

One of the consequences of ethnic diversity is that there is an extraordinary proliferation of places of religious worship: the Church of England, Catholics and Methodists, Lutherans, Rastafarians, Baptists, the Apostolic Pentecostal Church, the Church of the Assembly of God, the Church of God of Prophecy, the Seventh Day Adventists, the Chinese Church, Sikh temples, Synagogues, Hindu places of worship, faith healers, and obscure evangelical sects whose temples are often little more than corrugated iron shacks. Here the Lord speaks in an estimated forty tongues. When a famous Chilean evangelist held a series of prayer sessions at a local football stadium, he drew audiences averaging ten thousand a night, and buses and coaches were hired to take people from all over the Borough, to bear witness.

In the supermarket checkout lines, by the bus stops brimming over with women laden with shopping, in the winding queues around the post and DHSS office—the muttered prejudices and whispered insults come as a reminder that people cannot be legislated to love one another. However, the public picture is that community relations have been largely harmonious. Loud music, noise, and children running wild—these are the main reported causes of friction among people from different groups, as they are virtually everywhere else. The frequency of incidents of racial harassment and attacks was not monitored by the Council's Housing Department until the mid-1980s.

Strength in numbers and a 'hard' reputation mean that black youth in the area have little or no experience of racial harassment by their peers. But the public picture of racial harmony is deceptive. Asians have been the main targets for successive waves of street robberies, and rumour has it that most of the perpetrators have been black. Asian shops and businesses are also preferred targets for robberies. Sometimes the harassment of Asian people takes a more organized form. On one occasion a group of thirty youths, black and white, assembled outside the house of an Asian family, threw rocks at the windows, and chanted 'kill the Pakis'. This scene was repeated several times on council estates throughout the 1980s.

Nor is everything entirely harmonious within the various group-ings that make up the Asian community. There has been tension within the Sikh community, for example, exacerbated by the inflamed politics of the Punjab. One summer afternoon the patrons of the Central Library were startled to discover a full-scale street battle being conducted around the steps of the building. There were a hundred fully armed—swords, knives, machetes—members of rival Sikh gangs: the Billi Brothers were entertaining the Holy Smokes. Periodically, also, 'a good punch up' is reported between older black and Irish men, 'trying to settle who is the hardest'. One summer night, outside a still predominantly Irish private drinking club, shovels, pickaxes, and lumps of masonry were employed by both sides to emphasize their case.

4

The Satellite

'WELCOME TO SOWETO'—so read the stickers that festoon a
dank, communal stairway in one of the six greying tower blocks that
comprise the Satellite Estate. Each block contains some 160 apartments. There are also seven medium-sized blocks containing 652
living units, and 171 three-storey terraced maisonettes. Community
leaders often assert, and the impressionistic evidence supports them,
that this neighbourhood contains one of the highest concentrations
of people of African–Caribbean descent in the United Kingdom and
Europe.

The Satellite Estate was designed in the late 1960s. The architects
had dreamed of a quite different social tableau. They had imagined a
network of structures resembling cylindrical space capsules and
observation towers, connected by a criss-cross of aerial walkways.
But bit by bit the dream has been dismantled. Following a series of
muggings and assaults, the aerial walkways were pulled down, and
residents now use earthbound muddy pathways that intersect the
threadbare lawns. What vision of the future did these planners hold?
The multi-storey car park, designed to look like a series of lunar
docking bays, proved redundant to the needs of a poor community in
which 85 per cent of households had no access to a motor car—an
example, perhaps, of the ignorance of actual poverty which the
visionary designs of the Sixties planners concealed. The elevated car
park has now been demolished. Even the high-tech Estate Postal
Centre has been removed, and postal workers have ceased to deliver
registered letters or DHSS mail.

According to the Council, the Estate houses between seven
thousand and eight thousand people. But Council officials admit
that, in truth, nobody knows how many people live there and who
they are. After spending many hours visiting homes on the Estate, an
enumerator working on the 1991 UK Census stated that, 'Many
people would not answer their doors to me, although I could see that

they were in. I never realized before how much people live in fear of crime.' Another census worker stated, 'I came away with a feeling of sadness for people having to struggle to survive. There were men and women bringing up children on their own—all very fearful of the future.'

The high concentration of black residents resembles the segregated high-rise public housing of Chicago or New York. Many residents suspect that the tower blocks are used by the Council as a dumping ground for poor black people, single-parent families, and the mentally disturbed. A report into housing in the Borough claimed that black people were twice as likely as whites to be placed on large estates. It also took longer for black people to be rehoused from these estates. The report pointed to the gap between the Council's anti-racist policies and its practice. Racism in the Housing Department, the report concluded, took the form of inefficiency and poor service delivery.

One in three of all people in the United Kingdom lives in council housing. In Inner London and other inner-city areas, the proportion is over 50 per cent. In South Borough it is over 80 per cent. Most mass housing estates are bleak and forbidding places on the outside. Their size and architecture give them an institutional character, which is often made worse by the squalor of the lifts, the walkways, and other public areas. It should be stressed that some residents still manage to maintain immaculate homes which are as different from each other as the personalities of the tenants themselves. But for most residents, pride of place stops at the front door. In 1988 a survey of residents of South Borough found that 80 per cent of respondents wanted to leave.

The notion of empowerment of disadvantaged communities enjoys widespread support across the political spectrum. But politicians can often sound blithely optimistic about the organizational resources of poor neighbourhoods. The idea of enabling legislation to help communities control their own affairs counts for little when people are busy surviving from one crisis to another. Election-campaign pledges to improve the quality of neighbourhood life have a limited impact when the desire of many residents is to move out as quickly as possible.

In South Borough some local action groups were run by people from established church and voluntary organizations. The Revd Phil Blair, vicar of the Anglican Church of St Mary's in the Field, instigated a number of befriending, caring, and support groups over the years, involving the elderly, the disabled, the mentally disturbed, and mothers with young children. St Mary's Church is a vast, Victorian, Gothic building, perched at the summit of a hill of suburban streets. Once it dominated the landscape; now it is hopelessly dwarfed by the tower blocks.

In the afternoons, different groups of parishioners would meet for 'tea and sympathy' with the Revd Blair, in the modest front room of his rectory, a neat, chintz-curtained, semi-detached hive of neighbourhood activity, adjoining the church.

A more radical version of Christian action was initiated by the Borough's own turbulent priest, the Revd Vic Groves, a balding, motorbike-riding, phenomenally energetic minister who wore a bright silver crucifix over his leathers. Groves divided his time between local campaigns and a host of left-wing and anti-racist causes. He was active in the movement against apartheid in South Africa, and, through his association with the World Council of Churches, he had links with the African National Congress and other anti-colonialist independence movements in Africa and the Americas. He brought a third world, internationalist perspective to parish pump politics. For example, he arranged for the US Civil Rights leader and Presidential contender, Jesse Jackson, to preach at the local Methodist church.

Other groups were set up by the type of community activists described in one study as 'young, well-educated, middle class, and socially and politically committed' (Knight and Hayes 1981: 91; see also Butcher *et al.* 1980)—people who are undaunted by the prospect of spending every evening at meetings, and are prepared to make sacrifices to achieve their goal, whatever the cost. There was little involvement of the poor and disadvantaged in leadership positions.

Very few groups were truly indigenous to the community, in the sense that they were 'formed by people . . . directly affected by the problem that the group was set up to solve' (ibid.). Local trade-unionists during the industrial disputes of the 1970s had already proved that workers could organize their own struggle at the point of production. A key objective of many community activists, therefore, was to encourage similar attempts at self-organization outside the workplace. This meant challenging the domination of community campaigns and organizations by middle-class 'professionals'.

The professionals—the corps of Council-trained and funded Community Development Workers—were armed with a sociological training, and intended to be a long-term presence in the area. They operated with a much more sophisticated strategy than the *ad hoc* activists. The eventual defeat of militant strikers had also pointed to the limits of popular self-organization unsupported by broader social institutions.

Hence the professional ideology of the Community Development Workers aimed at building an organizational structure capable of supporting attempts at local self-organization. This structure was then supposed to act as a kind of intermediate bureaucracy between local government and the people. 'Community workers are committed, structurally, and whatever their personal politics, to a kind of Fabianism from below' (Robins and Cohen 1978: 27). In South Borough, Community Development Workers co-ordinated local groups though a network of Neighbourhood Forums. A series of reports were then produced by 'working parties', on issues such as housing, play space, roads, and public transport.

But, despite its sophistication—and its sophistries about the participation of local people—this form of community development remained essentially opportunistic. At the beginning of the 1980s most community organizations were formed by outside agencies. Or they were the domain of paid, professional community workers, full-time employees of the local authority, such as Randall Butterworth.

In the middle of the Satellite Estate a bunker-like compound nestles at the foot of a tower block. This is the 'Neighbourhood Project'. Randall Butterworth, a Senior Community Worker employed by the Council, was for ten years the Project's leader. During office hours Randall and his colleagues at headquarters ran an 'open surgery', providing information and advice about housing matters. Counselling and support were also offered for tenants suffering from a variety of psychological problems brought on by living on the

Estate. Randall also campaigned for better community facilities. After a protracted battle with the local authority, he secured funds for a much-needed working women's nursery/crèche on the Estate. He also initiated regular meetings of the Tenants' Association and, as its sole paid co-opted member, was responsible for the proper conduct of elections to the Tenants' Committee. He was also secretary and convenor of the Neighbourhood Forum.

Many tenants saw him as a vital intermediary between them and the Housing Department. But others labelled him as 'an ineffective, middle-class, do-gooder in granny specs, sandals, and Fair Isle sweater'. And, despite his best efforts on behalf of the children of the Estate, his office was broken into countless times—as often as once a week during the school holidays. Still, he was mostly well liked and generally popular. He reckoned that his main achievement after ten years was to have become an accepted part of the local scenery. Randall admitted that the post of chief community worker on the Estate is 'a tough and by and large thankless task'. A Methodist lay preacher in civilian life, he was sustained through many trials by his strong personal faith. Yet few of his clients and associates knew that he was a practising Christian.

The tower blocks look as though they will last a thousand years. Randall came to the conclusion that 'they are unfit for humans to live in. The only solution is to tear them down.' He recognized that, for all the solidity of the architecture, the Satellite was, in a human sense, an unfinished place. This futuristic estate was created at the whim of the planners, and entirely populated by newcomers—how to establish a true sense of harmony and co-operation here? Besides, one of the major obstacles to the establishment of community appeared to come from a minority of intensely disruptive juveniles and young men. As Randall put it: 'There are young people living here who act as if they are quite beyond the control of their parents, their schools, and even the police.'

Randall spoke about juvenile crime on his 'patch' with quiet despair. 'If your flat gets broken into, the first person you suspect is your neighbour, or someone close. Most likely it is someone you know who did it.' The most likely perpetrator of a street robbery will be a young person between the ages of 10 and 18. They are also the most likely victims (see Pratt 1980). As Randall Butterworth

The Satellite

sees it: 'Round here everyone steals off everyone else. It's a form of barter really, a world of its own.'

One night fire broke out in one of the tower blocks. The whole Estate was enveloped in thick black smoke. A man out walking his dog groped his way to a call box to dial 999. He sensed someone creeping up on him in the night and smog. He was grabbed from behind by the throat as his attacker tried to steal his wallet. While frightened, choking tenants were helped to safety by Randall and his colleagues, and the Fire Brigade battled against the blaze, items of clothing were stolen from the fire engines, and a television and other valuables were taken as thieves ransacked evacuated flats.

5

Bad Boys

YOUTH crime on the Satellite Estate during the early 1980s was rarely a matter of residents being systematically terrorized, caught in the crossfire of drug-trade-motivated inter-mob rivalry, as is common in the United States, and has started to occur in some of the inner cities of the United Kingdom. Instead the picture is of small gangs, some of whose members are as young as 12, engaged in various kinds of petty crime.

The pressure to survive means that only a low level of mutual trust can operate even among small groups of 'friends'. Friendship networks often function as false communities of mistrust, with depressingly high reported incidents of 'mates' stealing from each other and from the homes of their friends and neighbours. In such a climate, a boy has to undergo a process of premature toughening if he is to survive. His first lesson is not how to live in the family but how to negotiate the unstable society of his peers. And, having absorbed as a child the erratic values and attitudes of the subculture, he may remain trapped within it, psychologically paralysed, unable to break out, even if the opportunity were to arise.

Sammy Brown, 21, is stranded on the Satellite. He lives alone in a second floor flat in one of the tower blocks. He has lived there since he was a child. He remembers how pleased his mother and sister were when the three of them first moved into their clean new home. But now the rest of the family has departed. Last summer mother and sister went on a holiday to visit relatives in Jamaica. They did not return to the apartment. So Sammy took over the living-room of the two-bedroom flat; it contains a bed, TV/video, and sound system; on the wall is a poster of Shabba Ranks, the celebrated 'ragga' star. A quiet, handsome young man, with a somewhat sullen air, Sammy has a street reputation for being seriously hard, with an explosive temper to match. He claims, like everyone else he knows, that he would rather settle disputes with his fists, and that he carries a blade for protection only. His offending history includes a stabbing during a fight between gangs of youths from rival areas, outside a ballroom in the city centre.

There followed a charge of assaulting a police officer after a music concert, the police version of which Sammy denied, but he got sent down none the less. Sammy has spent much of his youth either skirmishing with the Law, or doing his share as 'a soldier' in a loose-knit neighbourhood 'posse', defending imaginary Kingdoms of the Street.

His employment history consists of a year 'on the NACRO'—one of the job-training schemes sponsored by the National Association for the Care and Resettlement of Offenders. This was followed by a brief spell on a Government Employment Training programme. But he remains largely unskilled, and has never been able to hold down a job for longer than a few weeks. It always 'got boring' or he felt he was being exploited and being treated 'like a mug'. Sometimes he would stay with the mother of his 3-year-old daughter who lives on the other side of the city. Sometimes he hung around Randall's Neighbourhood Project office. Or he would visit the Borough Law Centre, where he would aggressively harangue the staff to proceed on his behalf against the police for an incident which he claimed constituted harassment and wrongful arrest. As a result perhaps of his increased social isolation and lack of confidence, his behaviour became steadily more bizarre and unpredictable. Following a quarrel with his girlfriend over access to his daughter, he was persuaded to see his GP, who prescribed a course of tranquillizers and referred him to a hospital psychiatric unit. He failed to keep the appointment.

Although seemingly independent, and projecting a heavily macho image, many young men known to the police for petty offences, or deemed 'at risk of offending', are acutely vulnerable psychologically and depend on women for forms of care and comfort not dissimilar from child care.

Stuart Walters, 20, is a light-skinned black youth whose mother is white. He is plump, and baby-faced, with a demeanour best described as 'tired'. His speech is slow and deliberate. He was classified as 'borderline ESN' (Educationally Sub-Normal) at school. His employment history consists of long periods on the dole,

interspersed by enrolment on various Employment Training programmes, and spells of paid unskilled labour. 'This man gives me a
tenner to clear up for him like.'

Stuart appears to have given up on an early ambition to become a
tiler and pavier. Instead he gets up late and watches a lot of television
during the day, including Children's ITV. The household rents a Sky
satellite dish, like one in five of their immediate neighbours. But in
the evenings and at weekends, he enjoys an active social life. He has
a long-standing white girlfriend, to whom he has been formally
engaged for some time, and who wears his engagement ring.

Stuart was a keen soccer supporter, and regularly visited his local
club as part of a posse of 16- to 21-year-olds. Inside the ground they
would join the other supporters on the terrace and 'form up into one
big mob behind the goal'—the Borough Boys. Stuart was very
proud of 'my little posse'. But sometimes their activities ranged
beyond football.

There was this old geezer, and he was walkin in front of us, and one of us, I
dunno who said it—I think it was Liver, we take him for like our leader. He
said 'let's jump him', then he jumped him, then we all piled in like. And he
(the geezer) was on the ground. But when we went through 'is pockets, that
weren't more than 5p. It was ridiculous really. I said leave him alone now
like, we was all saying it.

Stuart's posse was eventually broken up by the police following an
impromptu post-match charge through a crowded street market.
Stuart is vague about the spells in detention centre and various fines,
probation, and community service orders that he has suffered. Both
he and Sammy Brown belong to the type of young offender referred
to by Job Restart counsellors to the unemployed as 'lacking in
motivation', by magistrates as 'the follower type who is easily led',
and by police officers as 'slag'. It is unlikely that Stuart could hold
down any but the most menial jobs, unless it is within a sheltered
environment. In the meantime, Stuart is sheltered by his womenfolk.

Paternal deprivation may well be the main cause of Sammy's and
Stuart's predicament. In the United States there have been studies
of black families which reveal statistical correlations between
delinquency, crime, academic failure, the inability to defer grati-
fication, and fatherless or disorganized homes. The life histories of

those youths such as Sammy and Stuart who came from matriarchal families and who have unstable or non-supportive fathers appear to confirm this connection. There are plenty of indications of the disintegrating impact on stable families, and on fatherhood in particular, of a dangerous social environment for youth combined with a harsh economic climate.

Yet there is also another kind of pattern among young male offenders in the neighbourhood: those, notably from the black community, whose family background is characterized by it conformity, orderliness, and the presence of a strong father.

In the West Indian parent culture, religion is the main source of conventions for a good family life and the ideals of respectability and personal responsibility. In South Borough there are fourteen Christian denominations. Some of them—such as the New Testament Church of God, the Seventh-Day Adventists, and the Pentecostalists—have wholly black congregations. The extraordinary determination of black churches in Britain both to survive and to grow is well captured in Anita Jackson's collection of conversations with black pastors in London. Over 90 per cent of church-going black people attend small inner-city black community churches (Jackson 1985: 136).

In a typically provocative vein, Daniel Patrick Moynihan once asked why black churches are neglected by radical reformers and social scientists. 'Do they not *really* reflect the energies and personal styles of the poor?', Moynihan asks. 'Or was it that the hymn-shouting and bible-thumping somehow does not elicit in the fancies of the white radical quite the same fascination as the black demi-monde?' (1969: 188).

The past decades have seen a steady decline in overall church membership in Britain. In the face of this trend, these West Indian—and African—congregations report regular increases in membership of up to 6 per cent a year (Jackson 1985: p. xv). One of the main contradictory facts about many high-crime neighbourhoods, therefore, has been the growing strength of the custom of regular Christian religious observance.

Byron Hilton's father is a respected deacon of his church. When Byron was a child, his father found it impossible to insulate him against the dangers and temptations of the street. He became prematurely streetwise. Short and stocky, he acquired the streetname Stumpy. In his father's words, 'by the age of 12 this Stumpy had seen too much'. Like so many of the West Indian parent generation, the Hiltons are bitter about what they see as the failure of the English educational system. Black youngsters, they feel, are not pushed to achieve academically, and there were far too few black teachers to act as role models. As Mr Hilton put it, 'Your schools failed our children.'

Mr Hilton embarked on a personal crusade among the youth of the neighbourhood. He visited youth centres, and spoke with club leaders about his deep concern for people such as his son. 'There is a nest [of wrongdoers] somewhere, I do not know where,' he exclaimed. 'But I shall find the nest and he can still be saved.' Instead, at age 16, Byron was sentenced to youth custody for the first time in connection with a street robbery committed together with another neighbourhood youth. On his release, Byron put on a characteristic display of repentance and remorse before his grief-stricken father, while at the same time engineering his unilateral independence from the family. (His parents also found out that he was bisexual.) In such contexts parents tend to become resigned to failure, retreat from painful confrontations (they might feel physically intimidated), to abandon their children, or even to take the initiative and eject them from the home. Of course, none of these options is solely the preserve of black parents. One white youth whose family sets great store on being perceived as respectable and law-abiding described how: 'I come 'ome one day and my bed was in the skip! My step-dad done it. He says it's 'cos the Old Bill came round the house looking for me. After he spoke to them, he just done 'is nut and that were it.'

Byron Hilton's parents, however, decided on what they saw as a more positive option, and one specifically available to people of Caribbean origin. Playing on his apprehensions about a further criminal charge, they bought him a one-way ticket to their home island of Jamaica, with strict instructions not to return! His father explained that they took this initiative because they were convinced that it was 'England that had done this to the boy'.

Byron Hilton's family is by all accounts a haven of the traditional virtues. The family of Ian Holder, however, shows how sometimes criminal activity, far from being learnt from the street, can originate within the bosom of the respectable family itself.

Ian's family, which came from Grenada, was related to Maurice Bishop, the deposed and murdered leader of the ill-fated New Jewel Movement. His father had risen to the rank of a senior manager with London Transport. Ian has not been heard of either by family or by friends, for four years. (There was an unsubstantiated rumour that he was dead.) For several years, Ian, who was regarded both by his parents and by his teachers as a sour and spiteful youth, was locked in a state of vengeful competitiveness with his older sister, who was described by her parents as an angel. She was the head prefect at her school, and went on to obtain a highly paid secretarial job. According to Mr Holder, in her final year of school, his daughter assiduously saved up all the money she had earned from weekend jobs, so that she could go and visit her relatives in Grenada. Ian, who had left school without any qualifications, stole the money from his sister, and spent it, so his father alleged, on drugs and gambling. Against all the evidence, Ian refused to admit his guilt, and instead took to barricading himself in his darkened bedroom, where he would sit for hours on end, listening to music and playing his guitar. Things came to a head when, following a charge of shop-lifting, Ian was physically ejected from the house, together with all his belongings. Despite attempts by his father to inform him of his mother's subsequent death, Ian has not been in contact with his family since his eviction. The syndrome of escalating and some-times pathological sibling rivalries is another common theme among families of young offenders in the neighbourhood.

There are also young people who come from acute criminogenic families. First, there are the children of professional villains, those who are from families where criminality is an occupational tradition. The pressure on them to take up crime is akin to the pressure to go into the family business.

Secondly, there are those who come from criminogenic families which are less stable, where chaotic displays of emotionality, and violent intrusions into each other's lives, may be the order of the day. Larry Sanchez's natural father is serving life imprisonment for murder, and his stepfather is a convicted armed robber. When he wished to show solidarity with his father, he both wrote to him and visited him in prison. At other times he attempted to blot him out and adopt his stepfather's name. Both Larry's and his older brother's skirmishes with the Law as juveniles originated out of their confusion and distress at the hurt that had been done to them by their family.

The member of a criminogenic family who feels that a primary injustice has happened to him because of his family, and that he has been harmed by it, may seek a vengeful solution. It is probable that the episodes of criminal vindictiveness of the kind displayed by Adrian Addison take place when he is in a private mood of bitter and agitated despair, as if the harm done to him, and the loss that he has suffered in his family, can only be undone by the law of talion— an eye for an eye—and through violent redress.

Adrian is a light-skinned black youth. His mother abandoned him, together with his older brother, when they were infants. They spent their early years in children's homes. Their natural father remarried and took the boys to live with him in a flat on the Satellite Estate.

When Adrian was 12 his father was imprisoned for a serious assault upon a neighbour—the result of a series of domestic disputes to which Adrian and his brother were witnesses. When Adrian was 15, his brother Lee, to whom he was very close and whom he idolized, was sentenced to life imprisonment for murder. Adrian spent a lot of time composing letters and poems and making drawings to send to his brother, and planning prison visits.

Outwardly there was little about Adrian to suggest such a tragic history. He was an extremely stylish youth—outsize 'bomber', £70 Reeboks, ear chains, LA Bloods cap set askew over a semi-mohican haircut—all this accompanied by a laid-back and dreamy manner. Adrian was also respected by the local youth—who knew him by the street 'tag' Blood. He was a master of hiphop, body-popping, and other dance techniques associated with the New York-based rap style of music. He could perform incredible feats of bodily control. He could spin on his head, an extraordinary sight! Adrian reached the final qualifying round of a prestigious hiphop contest organized by a national newspaper. To his chagrin, he was eventually beaten by a 14-year-old girl.

There was another side to Adrian. At the Youth Training Workshop which he attended, a pattern of vindictive and cowardly reprisals against anyone who annoyed or bettered him began to emerge. A supervisor who reprimanded him found his car tyres slashed. A trainee who annoyed him found his craft project destroyed, and so on. There was also a pattern of unexplained thefts. Adrian was finally dismissed from the Workshop following a blatant attempt to snatch a pile of wage packets from the office. Although he was a sprinter, he 'legged it' into the arms of a supervisor.

Unemployed, bored, and bitter, Adrian spent his time wandering around parks during the day. Then one evening he attempted to rob a 16-year-old Asian female school student by cutting the strap on her shoulder bag. This time his turn of speed might have secured his getaway, but, although she weighed less than seven stone and was only five foot tall, she managed to hang on to him until help arrived. She got an award for bravery. Adrian got eighteen months.

After his release, Adrian was 'signing on' for the dole, and looking for a permanent place to live. An attempt to perform his body-popping routine on the lucrative city centre circuit did not work out. His addiction to amphetamines had made him a scary person to be around. He was finally banned from the circuit after a fellow performer found his guitar damaged. He had not had an easy time in prison and remarked chillingly, 'Someone's got to pay for all that grief.' Then he dropped out of sight.

In Adrian's case a criminal career may have been inevitable and may be traced back to a painful family history. Nevertheless a distinctive feature of young black offenders is the incidence of those who are not drawn from problem families. Behind the simple label 'young offender' lies a far more differentiated picture.

Nevertheless, it is noticeable that many of the biographies of young adult offenders have a pattern about them, sometimes described by criminologists as 'crime career trajectories'. As Philip Cohen has observed, this phrase conjures up a picture of people firmly in control of where they are heading, and consciously choosing a deviant career structure.

But it would probably be more accurate to call it a *careering* structure. The young person may nominally be in the driving seat—after all it is his car— but in fact he is being given a whole set of contradictory instructions by a large number of back seat drivers, some of whom are selves, some of whom are others. Although everyone may think they are in control, the car itself is quite out of control, and often finishes by crashing into a dead end turning (brick wall?). (Robins and Cohen 1978: 162)

Luke Malone is an example of this careering process. His fate as a convicted criminal, rather than being virtually predetermined, is always in the balance. Luke's story also contains an important Irish subtext to the story of the neighbourhood.

At the age of 17 Luke was a tall, garrulous, likeable fellow. He bore a remarkable physical resemblance to Lofty, a character in the television series *EastEnders*, and this became his nickname at school. Luke came from a family prominent in the strongly Republican Irish community in the Borough. His mother was an active campaigner for the Republican cause. One of his uncles, reputedly in 'the Volunteers', was detained in the Maze Prison when Internment was first introduced in Northern Ireland in 1971. His father, a construction worker, was killed in an accident at work when Luke was a child.

Luke professed to be proud of his background. He could be vociferous in his defence of the militant Republican movement. 'I don't agree with blowing up people, but they should get the troops out.' Yet he himself had never set foot in Ireland, spoke broad cockney with no trace of an Irish accent, and would happily mimic an Irish brogue, refer to people from the Republic as 'bog Irish' and mock their superstitious Catholicism. One of his favourite dares as a schoolboy was to run into the bar of one the many predominantly Irish pubs in the area, shout 'Paddy bastards!' and hurriedly withdraw.

Luke enlisted in the local construction training workshop as a trainee carpenter, after his family's attempts to find him an apprenticeship through contacts in the building trade did not work out. Often the whole sense of self-esteem of a lad from Luke's background would be bound up with mastering a set of manual construction skills 'so as to become a tradesman like your dad'. But from the start Luke showed an almost total lack of aptitude 'on the tools'. His instructor reported that he displayed little inclination to improve.

Instead, Luke seemed to be unconsciously bent on fitting the English stereotype of Irish fecklessness, a central feature of the deeply ambivalent attitude towards Irish workers long held by both employers and fellow workers in England. In this basically racist ascription, Irish workers, 'the Paddies', are supposed to display little ambition or desire to improve.

Yet Luke could also be imaginative and thoughtful. His curiosity and anarchic sense of humour, coupled with his undoubted intelligence, clearly did not match the stereotype. Rather it pointed to a confused young man who did not know what he wanted, where he was heading, and whom he was supposed to listen to.

Luke's mother, a forceful woman, sometimes accompanied her gangling 17-year-old to the workshop. She would explain to his instructors that Luke had been recognized by his teachers at his Catholic secondary school as 'intelligent but wayward. After his father died they found it hard to keep his attention.' Indeed his attention wandered to such an extent that he was hardly at school, and even managed to abscond from the truancy centre to which he was subsequently referred. Accordingly, a great deal of Luke's vocational training was aimed at getting him to turn up!

While at school Luke had formed a close friendship with two other lads of similar background and disposition, Michael O'Mara and John Connolly. Together they created a collusive and protective fantasy world of their own, based on their shared sense of anarchic humour—'We would spend hours just looking around the streets (enacting scenes from Monty Python). One time a copper comes up to us and asked us what we were doing. We just laughed at him and ran away.'

Just before dawn each Monday on Jubilee Corner in the Old High Road the builders' labourers gather, the smoke from their cigarettes curling in the early morning air. At six o'clock the gangers arrive in their transit vans and pick-up trucks, and hand pick the week's requirement of casual labour. On Saturday nights in the Old High Road, Mackenna's public house echoes to the sound of traditional accordion music, and the Shamrock Dance Hall is well attended. On Sunday lunch-times, while the church of St Gabriel the Archangel gradually empties, the older Irish men in their baggy blue serge Sunday suits, crotches nearly down to their knees, lean on the crash barriers at the corner of the street. Many of them can recall how as young men in the 1960s they had been recruited from Ireland to earn a desperately hard living as bricklayers and labourers extending the motorway network across Britain. A sixty-hour working week, often living on site in makeshift caravans, and receiving shabby treatment from the contractors and the police—all this forms part of their collective experience, an experience not dissimilar to that of their predecessors, the 'Irishers' and 'navvies' of the nineteenth century, who excavated the great earth valleys that accommodate the railways.

Some of the contemporary experiences of Irish workers are also not so different from the 1950s. Yet, although never entirely disowning their Irish roots, indeed even taking actual pride in them, the seemingly unchanging historical experiences of generations of Irish workers in Britain held little relevance to Luke Malone and his friends. Instead they preferred to connect to another cultural heritage. The three friends shared a deep fascination with the mods' lifestyle of the early 1960s. This was brought on after they had seen a video of the rock opera *Tommy*, which evoked the seemingly balmy days of youth-in-revolt, and appeared to legitimate the 'do what you want' attitude to life of the mods.

To these Anglo-Irish city boys, who were breaking with the occupational and cultural traditions of their parents, the words of Pete Townshend's 'My Generation', the adopted anthem of the brave new mod world of the 1960s, echoed like a prayer, with its invitation to throw off the millstones of old-fashioned loyalties of place, class, and religion.

> People try to put us down,
> Just because we get around.
> Things they do they sure look cold,
> Hope I die before I get old.

The trio travelled to mod revivalist scooter rallies in Southend, Great Yarmouth, Hastings, and other coastal resorts which were bastions of mod and rocker culture. The problem was that Luke was the only one to possess a scooter. The exaggerated pill-popping bravado of these mod neophytes would sometimes bring them into conflict both with older revivalists and with the police. Luke bore his fines for obstructing the highway with pride.

'A mod has got to fight the Law. That's what makes you a true Individualist,' he asserted.

Another favoured haunt was the Spread Eagle Pub in the Old
High Road. This was the meeting-place for a variety of Rock Revivalist groups—Mondays: Elvis night; Tuesday: Rockabilly; Wed-
nesdays: The Johnny Kidd Appreciation Society. This latter group,
consisting of mums and dads—average age 40, kitted out in drapes,
leathers, tattoos, sideburns, and pony tails—vied with the others for
the title of True Guardians of the area's rock 'n' roll heritage.
Johnny Kidd had been a one-hit rocker of the late 1950s, 'Shakin'
All Over!' A Leather-clad Elvis/Gene Vincent clone, he was killed
in a motorcycle crash (how else?). He was also a True Son of the
area. Legend had it that he had been a member of a feared hundred-
strong gang of 'Teds' which was eventually broken up by the police
during an epochal street battle in the mid-1950s. Recent skirmishes,
between mods and teds and other rocker sects, culminated in a so-
called Riot on the Underground, as it was dubbed by the tabloid
Press, when some two hundred mods decommissioned a tube train
carrying rockers from a stadium concert, causing so much damage
that the train had to be taken out of service.

Luke's and friends' evening in the Spread Eagle would more
typically be taken up with musical appreciation and sometimes
heated philosophical debate about what exactly constitutes a mod
individualist. Two essential ingredients, according to Luke, were a
preparedness to resist the Law, and a commitment to survive without
working. This implied a willingness to engage in a variety of petty-
criminal hustles. But this did not mean that Luke had a criminal self-
image. On the contrary.

If I had a fiver for every time I could have nicked something and didn't, I
would be a rich man. I am basically an honest sort of person. Straight up. I
ain't kidding! I don't rob old ladies, nick their handbags, things like that. I
don't climb into people's houses . . . I would never hit a woman in my life.
The last time I had a fight I was about five. What I have done is fiddles.
Everybody does it. And I will admit barnies with the Law, when some
copper starts taking liberties. If you really want to talk to a real thief, you
want to talk to Ettienne [a noted teenage villain], he is a 'teef' [mimics West
Indian accent]. I ain't got nothing against him. But he is a thief. He will nick
anything.

After a year of fitful attendance at the training workshop, Luke's progress in terms of acquiring skills had been minimal. But he had shown signs of taking a more realistic attitude to the problem of earning a living legally. He decided that he would never be able to accept the imposed discipline of working for someone else. He started to explore the idea of some form of self-employment. But the extent of his personal disorganization was still formidable.

Luke had a steady girl-friend, Debbie, a childhood sweetheart, to whom at age 18, unskilled and unemployed, he was engaged to be married. He took this date as his deadline for coming off the dole and 'going legit'. In contrast to Luke, Debbie was an efficient and resourceful young woman. She worked on the secretarial staff of a film distribution company. One day in the office, Debbie overheard the Managing Director complaining about the unreliability of the postal service, and issuing instructions to his staff to seek out a bike messenger service to handle the company's mail. Debbie took the initiative and suggested to him that he might like to consider contracting her fiancé, whom he had already met at the staff Christmas Party. The Managing Director invited the couple for a drink one evening after work to discuss the plan.

The Managing Director was a member of the post-war generation of working-class grammar school boys made good. He was also an active member of the Labour Party. He listened intently to Luke's description of the plight of unemployed school-leavers. He took a shine to Luke, and Luke reciprocated. 'He's just a great bloke. The stories he tells. He's just a terrific fellah. And he likes a drink.'

Luke was offered an exclusive contract to handle the company's delivery and message service, on condition that he set himself up as a proper business, properly equipped and insured, with at least three licensed bike messengers to cope with the expected workload.

It seemed as though Luke's luck had turned. Here was a genuine opportunity to 'go legit'. But there were problems. Luke's own bike was off the road. One of his prospective partners, John Connolly, possessed only a Honda 50, while Michael O'Mara did not even own a pushbike.

Luke approached a charitable trust for financial support. What was required was the completion of a form facilitating the payment by the trust of a loan towards the cost of properly equipping the proposed messenger service. But the agreement forms were never completed. Several months later Luke reported, 'I've been on heroin. I'm off it now thank God. It was terrible. I nearly died. There's this Indian restaurant on the High Road . . . If you wanna do another book, Dave, you should do it with me about heroin.' He scarcely mentioned his business plan, beyond commenting that 'they [the charitable trusts] should make the forms simpler. I mean be fair. All that stuff about cashflows.' Besides, his friend Michael O'Mara had dropped out of the venture. 'He's shacked up with his girl-friend,' Luke reported. 'He don't wanna job, not really. He ain't never gonna work.' Luke meanwhile had broken up with Debbie. It also emerged that he was in serious danger of going to prison for fine defaults.

He grew increasingly depressed and agitated. He spoke obsessively about his bad luck, and took to carrying around the lyrics from a John Lennon song.

> If you had the luck of the Irish,
> You'd be sorry and wish you were dead.
> If you had the luck of the Irish,
> You would wish you were English instead.

Later that year Luke's 'luck' finally ran out. He received sentences totalling two years' imprisonment for fine defaults, drug, and other offences.

Psychoanalysts would doubtless emphasize the untimely death of Luke's father as a key moment in his life history. There follows the inability to carry on the occupational tradition of the family, the idolization of potential father substitutes, such as the Managing Director. There is the escape into the adolescent experience of the previous generation (his father was a Belfast mod). There is the inability to see any project through, the self-destructive urge (heroin), the addiction to screwing up (petty crime), and above all the increasing and ultimately disabling obsession with his Irish bad luck (the Luck of his Father). Like the character played by Jack Nicholson in the movie *Five Easy Pieces*, Luke's personal incapacity may be due to the fact that he was robbed of a vital moment of adult communicative experience with his father.

And yet there are an abundance of compensatory factors—his loyal friends, his resourceful girl-friend, his strong and supportive mother, his personal qualities of intelligence and personality.

In recognition of the complexity of this young man's psychic needs, psychotherapy appears to be required, for example through organizations such as the Personal Consultation Services operated by some local authorities, which offer free long-term counselling and even full courses of psychotherapy to young people in distress. Whether Luke would have been prepared to make use of such an organization, were it on offer, is uncertain. One thing is clear. In Luke's case, as in those of so many of the young people described here, imprisonment is a grotesque irrelevance, both to his own needs, and the needs of the society that this 'legal therapy' is supposed to protect.

In most biographies of young offenders there is a moment of hope, however slight, where prison might have been avoided. But there are also those, often referred to by their peers as 'evil people', for whom, even with the benefit of hindsight, prison appears to be the only solution.

Glenroy has a permanent look of self-satisfaction. He moves among his mates as if enclosed in a fog of self-regard. He interrogates them about where they get their trainers, jewellery, and other personal accoutrements. He is fiercely competitive. 'If someone's got something I like, then I'm gonna have it too.' For Glenroy, the pursuit of status conceals a goal of doing others down. He does not like to feel bettered. Glenroy is one of those youths of the inner city who seriously resent being told what to do by anyone.

Psychologists have interpreted such traits of delinquent behaviour as part of a strategy to conceal a lack of self-esteem, and this may be so, in the sense that unmanageable childishness is a learnt strategy of personal survival, as if 'the individual is not strong enough or adult enough to achieve his goals in a legitimate way, but is rather like a child, dependent on others who tolerate his childish manœuvres'. (Rainwater 1970: 77).

Others live directly off women. Upon his emergence from detention centre for 'brickin' a Paki', Mustapha, aged 17, of Moroccan extraction, 'shacked up', with a single parent in her mid-twenties and with her own flat on the Satellite Estate. This was a useful base for Mustapha, trying to re-establish his presence in the neighbourhood after getting out of 'nick'. In the short term, the timing and mode of delivery of his partner's regular welfare payments were of special concern to him.

Sexual relations are about manipulating the other person. A few weeks later, 'I've got two girls working for me' was his proud boast. Mustapha typifies the type of sexual predator who likes to insinuate himself into the affections of lonely and vulnerable women in order to extort money from them, whether by 'having away' their DHSS giros, or through 'offering them out'—pimping. One of his targets was a 13-year-old girl who had run away from home and was in the care of the local authority. 'She's fit, I could make a lot of money out of her.'

Even moments of communal relaxation are at risk of disturbance by the sexual bullies and predators. On a sunny workless afternoon on the Parade, a group of youths are talking and laughing together. Then Glenroy decides to join them, in order to 'show up' a youth half his size for lying about his relations with a woman at a party: 'He claimed he got backshot off of her when he only got tit.' Then he grabs the youth's hat and tosses it to a henchman. Youths old enough to vote are incited by Glenroy into playing piggie in the middle with a friend's dignity. As the tension among the youths mounts, the escalating language of ritualized aggression and abuse reminds those who use it that exploitation is the general rule and some form of humiliation the inevitable outcome.

Then Glenroy's mother appears from the launderette where she works. Glenroy breaks off the tormenting, and calls out and gives her an almost flirtatious gesture of affection. His mother gives him an affectionate pinch on the cheek in return. Glenroy can do no wrong in his mother's eyes, and he often declares that he would kill anyone who messed with his mother. The sanctity in which mothers are held in the community accords with the real-life saintliness of many women who are forced to bring up children unsupported by men or by an extended family network. In return for such devotion, Glenroy's mother believes that her son is 'sweet on women, nothing more'. But physically Glenroy is no child. 'I was just trying to sweeten her up,' he claimed, in response to a charge of committing a rape on a young woman neighbour. But the woman told a different story in court, of how the sweet talk prepared the ground for pred-atory violent sexual assault. For Glenroy, sex on that occasion was like stealing any other commodity, where satisfaction depends on taking what you want instead of waiting for what is rightfully yours to receive.

In a warlike social atmosphere, such creepy characters, whose main survival tactic is to prey upon those weaker and less resourceful than themselves, come into their own and exert an impact on the moral and social life of the neighbourhood out of all proportion to their numbers. Indeed it is possible for a convicted pimp or rapist like Glenroy or Mustapha, operating on his own, to transform the whole moral climate of a neighbourhood. Their activities directly impede the development of community.

At the heart of Mustapha's and Glenroy's activities lies the capacity for duplicity. A striking characteristic of serious young offenders is the quality of deception they bring to social life. For many, lying is the first law of the street. On one level lying is a protective act. For example, when questioned by the police, it may be necessary to lie in order to protect oneself and others from incrimination, apprehension, and arrest. In this context the capacity to lie persuasively under pressure is an indispensable weapon in the armoury of personal survival. But at another, deeper, level, lying also reflects a conviction that the social environment itself is somehow malevolent and untrustworthy. This sense of a kind of ruthless presence 'out there on the streets' gives some individuals the feeling that they are obliged to lie in order to survive. Lying displays the level of the individual's alert paranoid vigilance in the face of seemingly overwhelming environmental dangers. For some offenders, lying becomes living, as if they feel alive only when they lie. In many accounts of neighbourhood street life, it is noticeable how a lying or mythical account of events brings the speaker to life in a way that a factual report does not.

Probation officers and prison therapists, through group sessions called 'Looking at offending', attempt to enable offenders to tell the truth, and confront the destructive consequences of their behaviour. But if such programmes fail to break the cycles of inner-city pathologies, then the time soon comes when members of the community themselves take stock of their desperate situation and decide to devise solutions of their own.

6
The Group

ON the Police Station wall hangs a photograph of a group of youths. Underneath is scrawled the caption 'THE LOCAL MAFIA'. In 1980 these young men had just been released from prison. But, on returning to their area, they faced a different kind of reception. They were invited by Robert Walsh, a young, dynamic, and innovative Council Community Development Officer, to act as consultants to a report on the realities of life on the estate where they had been brought up, the Satellite.

The development of the estate [the report states] has been a disaster and has managed to incorporate all the problems associated with high density high rise estates. The streets and walkways are a menace, an escape route for muggers and a playground for children with nothing better to do than hang out on the streets. Eighty per cent of the people are of West Indian extraction. Blacks, whites and Asians view each other with considerable suspicion and sometimes with outright hostility. People from the Asian community see themselves as the prime target for racist attacks.

The consultants to this report were all children of West Indian parents who had come to Britain in the 1950s. They had spent their childhood and grown up in South Borough together. Convicted street robbers, with several years' imprisonment behind them by their mid-twenties, they had been deeply affected by their parents' disillusioning experiences of living and working in England. The attitudes of three of them to their families' experiences are typical:

ANDY MASON. My dad was Jack of all Trades but he specialized in carpentry. He was getting peanuts really for what he had put into Britain, coming over here thirty odd years ago in the mid-1950s. And I realized that even though I was born in this country, there was no way I would slave out my guts to build up this country because I knew really what they had to offer, which was keeping blacks at the bottom of the pile.

ANTHONY HEATH. All our parents went through that. We were saying no way
are we going to go through that thing. The dreams our parents had. The
dreams we had.

Leon's parents had come to Britain from Jamaica. Fingering a deep
scar on the side of his nose, he recalled: 'I was never spared the rod
when I got out of line.' By the time Leon reached secondary school,
his father had drifted away from the family, but sometimes Leon
would 'go check out my roots' and look up his father, a regular
drinker in one of the few pubs in the vicinity which black people
frequented in numbers.

LEON REED. I seen what happened to my parents, and I promised myself that
I wouldn't end up like them. They came here, did all the shit jobs that
whites didn't want, and they ain't got nothing to show for it. For the
youth, the only thing we got is each other.

Despite their feelings of frustration and disappointment, the
Caribbean immigrants in the 1950s had been a generally conformist
and law-abiding section of the population (see Rex and Moore 1967;
Lambert 1970). One community elder described how, in the Caribbean, 'You don't get that kind of impudence from children that you
have here, because society there wasn't very permissive. It was total
respect for your elders. No questions asked. One of the first things
you were taught was to respect yourself and then to respect everybody else.' In contrast, some of the young men among the new generation chose an outlaw mode of existence that represented a
profound break with the conventional lives of their parents. Some
resisted all forms of parental control. As the community elder put it,
'Here, in England, when children reach a certain age, they don't
want to know you. They stand up with fists to you.' Andy Mason
and Anthony Heath describe how the Group searched for alternative
role models outside the family which were part fantasy, and set
themselves goals which were unrealistic.

ANDY. The gang was always together. And, you know, you watch the
movies and you wanna be a gangster. But the reality was we were living
paper gangster lives. It's not really real but you gotta keep up to it nevertheless. You gotta keep in with the fashions, you gotta put money in your
pocket. People were drifting in and out of prison, so the Group became
weaker or another moment it became stronger.

ANTHONY. When you are a teenager, you're saying, when I'm 25, I'd like to have a big house. You want to have all the things that cost money. But you're not thinking about how you're gonna really, you know, prepare yourself to earn money legitimately.

The urban ethnographer Terry Williams describes the criminalized youth he studied in New York, 'searching for dreams that most will never find' (1989: 133). Among the Group from the Satellite, a favourite shared dream scenario involved 'the perfect crime'. This often took the form of a fantastic stroke of luck, as when the would-be robbers happen to stumble on the keys to the safe, and just help themselves to huge amounts of money. This tale fits with a belief, central to the pull of crime among the young, that success in life is a matter of luck, and that the old-fashioned virtues of diligence, patience, and hard work are for the mugs (among whom they may count their parents).

Another powerful fantasy is the dream of 'the big one'. In this scenario, there you are, going robbing, going nowhere. Then one big job changes everything. The perpetrators undergo a total transforming experience. They are transformed both externally and internally by the arrival of great wealth and spending power, which in turn bring great personal happiness. Underprivileged youth everywhere exhibits a fanatical devotion and respect for expensive cars, clothes, and jewellery. This is perhaps not surprising when we know that the advertising industry makes its living out of exploiting people's seemingly limitless faith in the power of consumption. 'In advertising the advertised product usually promises to alter the subject's external environment and hence change internal mood' (Bollas 1987: 16). Young people with little education or experience with which to measure the true value of things are particularly susceptible to the promise of the internally transforming power of commodities.

Compared to such fantasies, schooling and education held little promise for the Group. The 1970s had seen the move towards the establishment of educationally subnormal (ESN) schools and disruptive units within the English schools system. Out of all proportion to their numbers, black children were being labelled under-achievers and disruptives. The suspicion grew in the community that the indiscipline and underachievement of black children had been

engineered (see Coard 1971). Following the publication of the
Rampton Report in 1981, which criticized black parents for not
taking an active enough interest in their children's education, the
Chair of the Borough Community Relations Council countered by
stating that black parents had become disillusioned with the education system and warned that, 'if things do not change, then blacks
would start thinking of setting up their own schools.'

Among the members of the Group there were complaints that
school had failed to equip them with socially useful skills, and had
left them instead with a strong feeling of being ignored, however
hard they had tried to adapt to its norms. Lincoln Fredericks recalled:

They wasn't doing nothing for us at school. In history they was teaching us
about all white people like Christopher Columbus, who was nothing but a
liar and a thief, teaching us about evil people and making them our heroes,
so that was just rubbish. We didn't know nothing about ourselves, our own
people, our own heroes.

From childhood, Lincoln Fredericks was the acknowledged leader
of the Group. Tall and powerfully built, and always wearing a
black leather peaked cap, he was the most outspoken. This earned
him the nickname 'The Mouth'. For Lincoln, all the well-intentioned
exercises in multicultural education instigated by the local education
authority could not mitigate the impact of the realization of growing
up in an emphatically white culture where the angels are always
coloured white and the devil is always painted black, where a bad
day is a black day, where you do not get whitemailed, you get black-
mailed, and where even Tarzan, the King of the Jungle in Black
Africa, was a white man.

In other respects, however, the Group's shaping experiences were
identical to those of their white working-class contemporaries: a
familiar story of nothing to do and nowhere to go for the youth in
post-war urban England; no local cinemas, clubs, or sporting
facilities: 'You could mug, pick a purse, hang loose, gamble, smoke
weed, get drunk if you had the money. ' Yet Robert Walsh and other
community workers who came into contact with them were aware
that what distinguished Lincoln and his Group was that they
possessed a gut understanding of the politics of what it is like to be

young, black, British, and from the inner city, and Lincoln and Leon in particular could also articulate that experience. Above all they were acutely aware of the economic disadvantage that lies behind the fact that in 1990, ten years after the Group came out of prison, there were still only a couple of thriving black businesses in the Old High Road, and that, of the dozens of pubs in the area, not one had a black landlord. Even the pub adjacent to the Satellite Estate had remained an Irish enclave, its decor green, and portraits of Dave 'Boy' Mcauley and Jackie Charlton on the walls.

At the beginning of the 1980s the black community did not only lack money. It was still groping towards the kind of organization and leadership which could give it real political clout. Meanwhile on the streets a picture was emerging of chronic youth alienation. Karen Roberts, the leading woman in the Group, described how: 'There were youth hanging round on the streets, being harassed a lot by the police. There were a lot of complaints going on. Just walking around talking to people you could feel the tension was building up. It was there.'

In an attempt to take the initiative on behalf of the community and help defuse the tension, the Labour councillor for South Borough invited the police to confront directly the grievances of the local youth. In the summer of 1981 three representatives of the local police assembled at the Estate youth centre on the Parade. The police delegation consisted of an experienced sergeant with several years' duty in the area, and two younger police constables. Several members and friends of the Group were in the audience.

The atmosphere at the meeting was stiff and formal. The three officers appeared to listen intently, their faces expressionless, as one by one their audience, consisting of some thirty youths, spoke of their frustrations. Many felt that they were being systematically picked on: 'Everytime I walk the streets, I have to look behind me in case a policeman is there,' one youth stated. Many complained about the attitude of the younger officers: 'They act aggressive to impress us.' Older officers, on the other hand, made an effort to be more conciliatory in their dealings with the young.

As the meeting progressed, the focus broadened from the police to the humiliations and indignities experienced by black people in a predominantly white society. A young man of 18, an engineering student at the local polytechnic, stated:

Once I went to visit my cousin in the country. As I was walking along the street I noticed that I was the only black and all the whites crossed over to the other side of the street when they saw me. A policeman came up to me and asked what I was doing there. I told him that I came to visit my cousin. But he did not believe me and took down my name and address.

One of the young police officers interrupted: 'This estate is well known as a place where there are a lot of robberies and muggings', he said, 'and the victims are often Asians and old people, and the culprits are often youths who are black.' A member of the Group replied: 'The whole world has chucked everything at us and sometimes some of us are forced into crime to have something because we have nothing.'

  Outside the meeting, a group of youths was less conciliatory. 'The pigs are the enemy. Don't meet with them. This war inna Babylon!'

In 1981 one event above all reinforced the black youths' feeling of victimization. In the words of Anthony Heath:

What was happening around us at the time in '81 was grim. There was the thirteen young black people that was killed in the fire at a party in Lewisham. That raised consciousness in people's minds. And there was a strong feeling about doing something about the situation we were in.

After lengthy enquiries lasting several years, the evidence is that the Lewisham fire was quite possibly a self-inflicted horror, which was started by one of the guests at the party, rather than by white racists, as many preferred to believe at the time. But what was undeniable was the media's callous indifference tinged with racism in the reporting of the tragedy. Linton Kwesi Johnson's poetic epitaph for the dead conveys the unifying, radicalizing effect of the Lewisham Massacre, as it became known.

> Almost everybody had to sympathise
> With the loved ones of the injured and the dead
> For dis a massacre that we come to realise
> It could have been me
> It could 'ave been you
> Fell victims to the terror by night.

In April 1981, following Operation Swamp—a campaign of aggressive saturation policing by the Special Patrol Group, in the course of which three thousand people were stopped and searched—Brixton erupted. Twenty-eight buildings and 117 motor vehicles were set on fire, and 279 police officers were injured. By the summer, rioting had broken out throughout Britain's inner cities, including Liverpool, Manchester, Leeds, Nottingham, and Leicester. Anthony Heath described 1981 as 'a crucial year'.

A group of us, we was driving around London. There was barricades in Brixton. Cars set on fire in Hackney. Every place we visited they was out on the streets. In Peckham there was looting. There were arguments with the police starting up everywhere we went. It was like the police was losing control. People call 1981 the year of the riots. But at that time it looked to us like an Uprising. And that's what we called it, an Uprising. It was like you see in South Africa, the revolution was starting.

There was also anger towards what many felt were self-appointed spokespersons for the black community. Some were employed by the Government-backed organizations, the Community Relations Council and the Commission for Racial Equality. A writer in a radical grass-roots newspaper stated: 'All the discredited political charlatans, masquerading as spokesmen of the black community, have emerged from their comfortable freehold homes to speak for the rioters.' Some of these spokespersons vigorously denounced the rioters and whole-heartedly condemned their activities, at the same time as calling for greater sensitivity to be shown by the police. Among some of the youth these 'community leaders' became known as 'professional West Indians'. The stage was set for a new leadership to emerge.

7

The People's Council

ALTHOUGH the area contains a high concentration of people of African–Caribbean descent, South Borough remained calm during most of 1981. 'There weren't nothing happening round there,' Andy Mason recalled. 'Everybody just going to jail, or coming out of jail as usual.'

In the wake of the riots, Lincoln Fredericks and the Group of youths from the Satellite formed themselves into the PC, the People's Council. Lincoln announced: 'We want to try and get people to do more constructive things with their lives.' Robert Walsh, Community Development Officer (and later Assistant to the Borough Chief Executive), was appointed by the Council to advise the Group.

The newly formed board of management of the People's Council was subjected to intense coaching in the rituals of committee organization by Walsh. He gave what amounted to a training course in committee procedure: the rules of the quorum, the importance of accurate minute-taking of meetings, the rights and responsibilities of chairmanship. This to an audience composed of young people who had had little formal education. Perhaps for the first time since they had left school, the members of the Group were presented with a middle-class model of 'how to behave in public'—a behaviourism in which they recognized the subjection of their own culture but found an apparent means of mastering their environment. If they could learn the bureaucratic ropes, they could handle the Council—and this, in turn, would increase their standing in the community.

So there was a group of convicted robbers, led by a man of considerable reputation on the streets, asking a white, middle-class university graduate about points of order and how motions were passed—exercises in painful deference to learning. In the long run, the ability to master the complexities of the Constitution, and to identify correctly the powers and functions of the various Finance subcommittees of the Council, was supposed to strengthen their position as community leaders. But its immediate effect was to strengthen the pivotal position of Robert Walsh, a danger which both Walsh and the Group itself were quick to recognize. Walsh recalled how:

On one occasion when I was working with the Group in the early days, I had written some chapters of a draft feasibility study. And I had really gone on a bit too quickly and started putting down a whole lot of my own ideas, and at an early meeting they were very critical and we had quite an argument because they felt that I was running away with the project. I learnt a great lesson that day, which was to ensure that reports and plans were their ideas, and that it wasn't my job to impose ideas on them. They decided what was going to happen, they decided how a community project was going to be run. The philosophy was that it should be run by the local community, that local people should be trying to run it.

What was at stake was the goal of empowerment itself.

The first headquarters of the People's Council was a disused garage on the Satellite Estate. It became a favoured meeting-place for the neighbourhood youth, many of whom were unemployed and had nowhere else to go except the streets. Inside the club was a deafening sound, the walls rocking to a pounding guitar bass. Knots of table-football addicts, with Afro-hairstyles, flowered shirts, and flared trousers, would occasionally break off their competition to engage in flirtatious banter with groups of young girls, who would be chatting and laughing together. The Club coffee bar was a makeshift affair of a couple of second-hand formica-topped tables, and the latest line in Youth Service chairs and sofas. An annexe housed a battered table-tennis table and a junior-size snooker table with a rip in the baize. At the club entrance was a makeshift noticeboard advertizing the services of Youth Advice, and the Neighbourhood Law Centre. A Drugs Helpline leaflet was pinned up alongside a Free Nelson Mandela poster.

Despite its poor amenities, the club was a lively place, never lacking for patrons, and relations between the organizers and their clientele were usually relaxed and marked by mutual respect. Lincoln and the Group displayed a genuine gift for communicating with the youth of the area. Through this club, the People's Council was building a popular base of support in the neighbourhood. But outside, on the streets, the violent tensions of the summer of 1981 had finally reached the area.

KAREN ROBERTS. I just happened to be outside the club at the time, and I noticed that a group of white skinheads came over to try and round up people to go rioting. One came into the club to see what was going on.

LINCOLN FREDERICKS. The club was just so packed, it just couldn't hold no more, and outside was just becoming packed, and there was this guy running up and down with a chopper saying he wanna chop up a bull, and another come up with a pickaxe, and they had all different weapons, and I'm just saying, 'Yeah, you know, them serious!'

KAREN. So I went up to one of them and said, 'What's the plan then, eh?' And he said, 'We got to go and get 'em', and I said, 'Who?', and he said, 'police', and I said, 'Where are the police?' And he said, 'Over there! We gotta get 'em before they get us!'

LINCOLN. I tell you someink. The community workers were telling us to go 'ome. These were the people they was telling us to go 'ome. They was saying, 'We can't do nothing. Leave them, they gonna riot. Get yourself out.' And they was supposed to be doing the job and keeping these people from rioting. I can't understand that.

KAREN. Something happened then. I just turned round and started saying to people, look, don't go following these people, 'cos at the end of the day it's gonna be in the newspaper headlines. 'Blacks Running Riot on the Streets', not 'White and Black Youths', but 'Blacks Running Riot'.

LINCOLN. 'Cos what we was saying to the youth was, 'We've started building something, right! And we don't want to destroy what we build. We just started doing something! If we "mash up" this place, we're gonna have to look at it tomorrow morning. If you gonna riot, go up Hampstead, go to where these people are OK, where when they go into the back garden its like 200 acres. Go to them places. What you mashing up your own place for?'

Lincoln Fredericks's reputation in the community changed dramatically. He became known as the person who had prevented a riot by the force of his personality and his argument that it made little sense to destroy what little local people had. The story of 'How Lincoln Stopped a Riot' spread far beyond the Borough. To many, it showed that the area was far from apathetic in the face of its problems. Stimulated by the Community Development Workers, the locality had thrown up not only the People's Council but a range of other grass-roots community organizations and spokespersons, which between them provided care for the elderly and the disabled, and set up black arts and cultural projects, including a popular reggae recording studio. Some of these activists were members of the Labour Party in an electoral ward where, as one councillor admitted, 'you could put up a sack of potatoes to represent Labour and it would get in'. However, the ideal of socialist unity was noticeably absent from community politics. This was a politically fractious and divided neighbourhood. A middle-aged woman office worker who lived next door to the Satellite Estate started a Stop the Muggers Campaign. She herself claimed to have been mugged several times by youths from the Estate. On one occasion, she claimed, a valuable item of jewellery had been snatched from her. On another occasion, 'when I refused [to hand over her valuables] he gave me this'—a pronounced scar runs down one side of her face.

The Stop the Muggers Campaign had a core of some four or five volunteer helpers, most of them middle-aged white women who lived locally. Professional community workers were not involved, indeed some were overtly hostile. The Stop the Muggers Campaign in its turn claimed to be the only truly indigenous community action group, operating free of council interference, in the neighbourhood. The Campaign's main activity was visiting and giving comfort to elderly people who had been attacked and robbed. In this respect, the Stop the Muggers Campaign was a forerunner of the Victim Support Groups. But the Campaign's claim that it visited the homes of several elderly victims of muggings a week was disputed by many as exaggerated. The Campaign also differed from the Victim Support Groups in that it extended its activities into a more controversial area than home visits to the elderly. At the height of a spate of street robberies, the committee organized a petition, which was signed by several hundred people, to bring the police Special Patrol Group into the area 'to deal with the muggers'. This was an inflammatory demand. The SPG's heavy-handed approach had fuelled the Brixton riot. It was hated and distrusted by large sections of black youth. Despite strenuous denials, wild rumours abounded that the Campaign was linked to far-right political organizations who were anti-immigrant. The Campaign was also rumoured to have the tacit support of the local Chief Inspector of Police, even though its call for deployment of the SPG had been ignored by him in favour of a reputedly more sensitive community-policing approach.

After the summer of 1981, while the various community groups struggled to establish themselves and competed for scarce local resources, another intervention was taking place, this time in the form of large, multi-million pound, Government programmes, managed by the Manpower Services Commission (MSC): The Community Programme, the Youth Opportunities Programme (YOP), the Voluntary Projects Programme—through these national programmes, a range of job training, counselling, and temporary employment schemes would be set up, with the aim of assisting the growing number of unemployed people. Area Manpower Boards—containing representatives of business, trade unions, education, and the local authority—were given the task of presiding over the implementation of these initiatives. A cohort of civil servants, with the job title of link officer, was dispatched by the MSC to co-ordinate matters on the ground.

The link officers recognized the severity of unemployment among the local youth, which was estimated to have risen to 80 per cent on the big estates. They were therefore prepared—or had been instructed from on high—not to scrutinize the content of schemes too closely, and to take a liberal view of funding arrangements, so long as activities started up quickly to deal with the immediate crisis.

Many projects were quite generously funded, at least at the outset. Sponsors were allowed to budget for the maintenance of low instructor–trainee staffing ratios. This was in recognition of what MSC policy-makers referred to as the 'special needs' of the youth of the area. Low staff–trainee ratios were considered to be an essential prerequisite for work with 'difficult' youth.

The arrival of the MSC did not go unopposed. There were those on the left of the Labour Party who saw every aspect of this intervention as further evidence of creeping centralism, with an accompanying dimunition in the power of the local authority, and they therefore urged that a Labour Council should refuse to co-operate. Many suspected that the Youth Training Scheme (YTS) was a cynical attempt by the Government to magic away those damaging unemployment figures. Also, MSC link officers had made it clear that their liberality would not extend to groups with professed radical political aims. This meant that programmes with an openly campaigning edge would have either to tone down their rhetoric or to tailor their objectives to meet funding guidelines. This was portrayed by the left as a covert form of censorship. Finally, according to these leftist critics, 'Life and Social Skills' training was being offered on YTS courses with the underlying aim of replacing the world of Big Youth Posse with more socially acceptable—to the establishment—attitudes, such as the acceptance of personal responsibility for one's actions, a concern for others, and, not least, a willingness to conform. And, in return for swallowing this establishment propaganda, these critics argued, the youth was given vague promises of new technology and improved training courses leading to upturns in the economy 'in the future'.

Despite these cavils, local-authority co-operation with the MSC was grudgingly secured, and most of the MSC-funded schemes for people out of work in the Borough were either proposed, sponsored, or managed directly by existing community groups. From the point of view of the MSC, these groups acted as convenient conduits for Government funds. From the point of view of the community organizations, MSC support meant that at least they were not solely dependent on the local authority, especially for their staffing needs. There may have been strings attached. But it did allow them to expand their activities.

The intervention of the MSC in community affairs threatened to have a major transformational impact. Skills Training Centres and the like quickly sprang up in disused factories, schools, and short-life housing blocks. But preparation for these schemes was often slipshod. The politics of youth unemployment required that schemes had to be arranged hastily, with very short 'lead-in' times. In many cases staffing of the schemes itself formed part of the Government's response to unemployment. Instructors were hired on short contracts for minimal wages, under the terms of the Community Programme, a temporary employment scheme for unemployed adults. There was little attempt to gear training to the needs of the local economy, and uncertainty about what would constitute the right kind of provision.

All these factors, combined with the suspicion and resentment of trainees who had seen their hopes of finding 'a proper job' come to nothing, meant that the quality and effectiveness of Youth Opportunities varied greatly, to put it charitably, from scheme to scheme.

The left's response to these developments proved ineffective. There were half-hearted attempts to unionize trainees, and sometimes a couple of men with beards and leather jackets would stand outside the gates of the New Start Training Workshop and try to flog copies of *Socialist Worker*. Given the chance, they would tell the youth that they were being exploited as a reserve army of cheap labour for capitalism.

The New Start Training Workshop was modestly housed, in an abandoned munitions factory opposite a gasworks. The Workshop catered for unemployed school-leavers and older youths with little or no work experience, including many who had been released from periods in custody in detention centres and borstals. Most of New Start's intake had a poor record of achievement at school. They were further disadvantaged in the job market by other factors—ethnic minority status, a record of offending, and so on. In recognition of these young people's special needs, as many as twenty staff were employed to take care of seventy trainees.

The New Start Workshop offered young people a year of basic training in one of the following: dressmaking, moto-mechanics, painting and decorating, sheet metalwork, bricklaying, plumbing, and catering. Instructors were chosen for their qualifications and experience in these areas, as well as in teaching and youth work. New Start's staffing policy included a central commitment to ensuring the involvement of people from the ethnic minorities. Some instructors were also experienced tradespeople recruited from the local labour force. Fitzroy Gains, for example, was a former US Marine in his fifties, born in Jamaica, who had previously owned his own joinery. He ran his sheet metalwork section with cheerful authority. Even the toughest and most uncooperative of the youths under his charge were fearful of overstepping the mark with Fitzroy. Legend had it that his steel toe-capped boots were not worn only for reasons of health and safety. The presence of instructors like Fitzroy, who were from the locality and who were experienced in their trade, gave trainees a taste of the real thing, as opposed to undergoing a paper exercise in vocational training.

New Start's trainees, boys and girls between the ages of 16 and 19, the majority of them black or Asian, who lived in the surrounding neighbourhood, had been unemployed since leaving school. Few had more than a couple of elementary examination passes to show for eleven years of formal schooling. Some of them had been diagnosed as 'remedial', or 'borderline ESN'. Others had been labelled 'disruptive'. Most had managed to pass unnoticed through the education system. Instructors at New Start spent much of their time teaching 17-year-olds such mysteries as how to read a tape measure, a non-digital watch, a road sign. Yet these were perfectly healthy youngsters with no record of mental or physical disability. Instructors often found themselves wondering what had been going on at school.

Among New Start entrants were those who had come straight from Borstal. Older looking, more streetwise than their contemporaries, the leather-coat boys, as they were known to the staff, frequented New Start as a safe hang-out, out of reach of the Law. Their activities often directly threatened the smooth running of the workshop. On one occasion Paresh, an earnest young man with hopes of becoming a computer programmer, was sent over to the Workshop from the Job Centre. On his first day he was invited to join a card school, and someone tried to sell him some 'dope'. An emissary of the leather-coat boys filled him in on the 'taxing' system. His hastily arranged induction session was sabotaged as staff rushed to intervene physically in an argument between some youths, in the course of which knives were brandished about.

Yet, despite the shabbiness, the sometimes chaotic organization, the presence of the leather-coat boys, and many other depressing features, New Start was a source of hope to these embattled youngsters. For the mainstream of school-leavers, a basic training at New Start could help them to move on, from being helpless kids, dependent on parental hand-outs and paper rounds, to being young workers, capable of holding down a job.

As for the 'Bad Boys', New Start was capable of helping them too. The Big Youth Posse may be 'massive' on the streets, but its members have a low sense of self-worth when it comes to the job market. The manager of New Start, Jack, was less hopeful about them. 'Teach them a skill? Make them useful members of society? The best you can say is that we are keeping them off the streets, so that they are not such a danger to the public.' As a former personnel officer recruited from the motor industry, Jack always wore a suit and tie, and preferred to keep to his office, aloof from the shopfloor. In his early fifties, from a northern working-class background, Jack saw himself as a tough realist when it came to the job market. 'You have to ask, "what good are these youngsters to prospective employers?"' He was nevertheless keen to implement the latest 'package' to emerge from the MSC Vocational Training Modular Design and Delivery Unit.

Worried about the financial cutbacks which invariably follow initial bursts of Government generosity, Jack spent a lot of time at Council meetings, lobbying for alternative sources of support. He tried to persuade civic dignitaries to visit the Workshop to witness its achievements for themselves.

Jack's second-in-command, Steve, was a sharp contrast. In his mid-thirties, with a definite *City Limits* presence, he had a genuine empathy for the cultural preferences of his trainees, and a marked antipathy to the pseudo-scientific 'time-and-motion' approach to youth training favoured by Jack: 'What trainees need are real skills, not endless assessment forms,' he argued.

Late one afternoon, after the last trainee had knocked off for the day, Jack convened a meeting of his staff. Quietly he announced that, following a decision of the Area Manpower Board, the number of staff was to be cut by half. This was in line with major Government cutbacks in funding for youth training nation-wide. But Jack had been tipped off by the project's link officer that this was the precursor to a complete withdrawal of funds. Several other training projects in the vicinity had already been forced to take the 'self-financing' option.

A strangely subdued debate followed Jack's announcement. Then, just as it threatened to become acrimonious, Jack terminated the meeting and the staff went home angry, yet defeated inside. While locking up the office, Jack's deputy, Steve, came across Wayne, the leader of the leather-coat boys, his faithful shadow Lloyd, and Mark, a trainee Steve had previously trusted. Mark tried to persuade Steve to hand over the safe keys: 'The others are all "tooled up". Why get involved? The place is gonna be closed down. This money is *ours*. Why get hurt to protect *them*?'

From his student days in the late 1960s, Steve's rejection of authoritarian institutions had been fuelled by a gamut of alternatives—from anti-psychiatry, to de-schooling. But over the years his revolutionary idealism had been tempered by hard experience. He remained distrustful of the political manœuvring that lay behind the implementation of the YOP and the YTS. He was aware that Jack's enthusiasm for 'personal effectiveness training', 'trainee profiling' and the rest was misplaced. He knew that behind all that extravagant theorizing lay the sad reality of thousands of young people in training for no jobs. A shabby con. But Steve would also vigorously defend the positive side of New Start's work, and was sensitive to the threat to it posed by the villainous elements among the youth. Long before the prospect of closure, Steve had been in conflict with his manager. Now, confronted in his office by youths carrying knives and prepared to use them, Steve's commitment reached breaking-point.

What did Steve do? In the actual incident on which this scenario is based, he raised the alarm and alerted the police. But the cynical view of Government programmes for the unemployed could just as easily have prevailed. One militant observer argued that community projects functioned as 'another means of keeping blacks helpless and dependent. It leaves nothing to risk and provides no structure for action—except in designing schemes to manipulate them advantageously. It is just another white man's game for which the black man must as always invent his own response' (Dodd 1978: 25, cited in Pitts 1988: 131). Other radicals have stated that crimes committed by blacks against whites are acts of resistance. (During the Brixton disturbances of 1981, a youth worker noticed a group of black youths breaking into a jeweller's shop. The youth worker urged them to stop. Back came the reply, 'This our gold man! It come from South Africa!')

Incidences of corrupt or imprudent handling of public funds by inner-city groups often stem from deep-seated cynicism about establishment motives. Sometimes this cynicism is matched by the providers themselves. One experienced member of the army of civil servants whose job was to monitor schemes for the unemployed complained:

It's a charade. We know that half of the reports we get from community projects are misleading. But we are not encouraged to scrutinize them too closely. The provision of public funds for the purposes of the amelioration of unemployment and providing vocational training—frankly it's political blood money. The cash the Government doles out to these projects is primarily intended to buy a bit of peace and quiet for the authorities. What else they achieve is quite another matter. Take the numbers game. Projects get funded according to the number of people they attract to their programmes. So everyone plays the numbers game. They would be stupid not to. But the reality is that I am quite used to scarcely meeting an unemployed person on some of these schemes. Some of them claim regular throughputs of hundreds of unemployed people. I seldom meet them.

During the 1980s Government employment schemes regularly reported cases of deliberate sabotage—incidents of supervisors' cars being wrecked, fire extinguishers deliberately let off, tools and technical equipment vandalized and stolen. Could temporary work and training schemes again become a focus for popular unrest? Lincoln Fredericks's angry oratory gave a powerful voice to people's feelings of distrust of Government schemes and their frustration with the sophistries of community participation:

Let's see some practical action. Let's see some serious practical help or aid to blacks and not dependency. Let's not see no Mickey Mouse blacks, let's not see no imagery no stereotyping, of black participation. Let' see some real assistance. Let it come truthfully. Once you keep lying, you get caught out. And that's when a riot comes, they feel like they're shocked, they're surprised. How could this happen? They gotta deal with it. If they don't deal with it, then they were forewarned and they didn't wanna heed it.

After the riots of 1981 the Government appeared to heed the warning and poured money into the inner cities. But at the same time, as a result of the riots, the black prison population expanded to record levels. In 1982, 23 per cent of the daily intake at Wandsworth jail was black. In April 1982, according to the Home Office 50 per cent of the population of Ashford remand centre was black.

Brixton (another remand prison) and Aylesbury prisons were between 25 per cent and 35 per cent black. So were Rochester, Dover, and Hewell Grange borstals and Blantyre House detention centre. Others with more than 10 per cent black inmates were Wormwood Scrubs, Parkhurst, Albany, Wandsworth, and Reading prisons and Wellingborough, Bulwood Hall, and Feltham borstals (Pitt 1988: 121–2). In the life histories of the street youth of South Borough, the débâcle of prison is a recurrent theme (for a moving and graphic account, see Hercules 1989).

One local youth describes his first experience of police custody:

I am directed to my cell by a police officer, well it's hardly directing more like a frog march. His eyes meet mine with a firm gaze. I look for a change of expression but no change appears. He points to my new home, given to me on behalf of Her Majesty the Queen. Then it hits me. I hear the sound of metal closing behind me. My cell door has been shut . . . I search for a luxurious bed and a chest of drawers . . . there is none of this. All I see is a hinged board about three feet above the ground, with a partition wall surrounding a toilet unit. I sit on my bed and sink my head in my hands. I want to cry, but I can't. I just keep rubbing my eyes. I think about my family. They don't even know I'm here. I think of how I got to be here. The cell is cold, and I try to keep warm by rubbing my arms violently. I guess I must have zedded, for I find a police officer, the same one that nicked me, shaking me. I glance past him and notice another officer standing at the entrance of the cell door. My gaze returns quickly to the first officer . . . He is taking out a notepad and a pen. I glance at his face, but I wish I hadn't. His face looks tired and drawn. The skin around his eyes is thick and red as though he had been working for weeks on end without rest. His beady eyes shift from side to side. I realize he is taking down a description of me, my height, my clothing. He begins to ask me questions. 'What's your name?' 'Where do you come from?' My answers are short and precise. I tense my body while speaking, as though expecting him to 'rumble' me . . . I have heard from people that the pigs are always slapping people when they suss that you are lying. After the officer has finished his questions he leaves the cell and once again I feel lonely. I hated these pigs coming around me, but somehow they eased the loneliness. My head begins to feel heavy and I lay back on to the hard bed. In my hand is a piece of paper. Some words are printed in big black letters and simply read, 'INTENT TO ROB'.

These words hit me very hard and for the first time I realize I have been charged with robbery. My eyes droop and I begin to shake. The tears have suddenly begun to appear in my eyes. I realize once again that I have been charged with a serious crime. I crumple the sheet of paper and throw it into a corner of the cell. I then leap under the covers they have supplied for the hard bed, as if I am trying to run away from the words. But I know I am not running anywhere. Nor are the words. For the words are here to stay.

At the end of this melodramatic and self-conscious description of his plight, this young man is filled with remorse. Yet before his arrest he took great pride in his status as an outlaw, and saw everyone as basically dishonest, or only honest because they feared the consequences. Only intense psychoanalysis could reveal the extent and intensity of his subjective experience of emptiness and isolation brought on in custody. Often the experience of prison accelerates people's sense of inevitability and hopelessness in contexts of personal defiance and defeat. But, for some black youth, prison produces a radical personal transformation.

Ronald came from an educated family, but his father, who had been a prominent trade-union organizer in Jamaica, had begun to be absent from the home. In Ronald's last school year he was stopped and questioned by police officers and charged with theft, handling, and possession of a small bag of 'sensi'.

Ronald seldom referred to his upcoming court appointment. When he did so, it was as though it was happening to someone else. Solicitors and probation officers would often advise their clients to join the local Youth Training Workshop. Perhaps the Bench could be persuaded that it could be a worthwhile point of referral in lieu of prison, as part of a probation order. Ronald appeared indifferent. But, when pressed about his motive for joining, he declared: 'the judge don't like it if you're unemployed.' His only request was for permission to 'chip' early in time to pick up his 2-year-old daughter from the nursery.

In fact 'bailing', and so avoiding nasty confrontations, appeared to be Ronald's *raison d'être*. A sly smile, a conspiratorial air, an affected look of wounded surprise when reprimanded—it soon became clear that his considerable sense of pride and self-esteem was located somewhere else; in his reputation among his peers as one who was worldlywise beyond his years, in community parlance 'a yout' who knows the runnings.'

I acted as a character reference for Ronald at the Magistrates' Court. Often my sense of these proceedings was that the invariably white and middle-class people who sat in judgment were either personally affronted by the exaggerated pride of some black youth, or (wilfully?) misread it as contempt for their authority. Ronald's obvious lack of respect for the court could not have been in his favour. He was sentenced to three months' youth custody.

After his release, Ronald returned to the training workshop, to the surprise of many people. Tests showed he was well above average intelligence. He was put under the wing of an experienced black senior supervisor in the electronics section, and he began to show good progress.

Years later Ronald reported that the experience of prison had fundamentally changed him. At the time of his incarceration, nearly half of his fellow inmates were black. 'Most of them just didn't seem to understand what was happening to them. They didn't want to understand. They were black yes, but they didn't know what it was to be black. They hated the police yes, but what they wanted was the "chop". They just love chop in South London.'

While in custody, Ronald fell in with a couple of Rastafarians from South London. These men were different. They were being treated with suspicion by prison officers and by some fellow prisoners. Their protestations concerning their religious needs—for example, a vegan diet—were being treated with contempt. A Home Office Circular to Prison Governors first issued in 1976, stated:

It has been decided that Rastafarianism does not qualify as a religious denomination for the purpose of section 10(5) of the Prison Act 1952, which requires a Governor to record on reception the religious denomination to which a prisoner declares himself to belong. Accordingly, if an inmate on reception wished to record Rastafarianism as his religion, he should be informed that he cannot be accepted for registration for the purposes of section 10(5) of the Prison Act 1952 and Rule 10 of the Prison Rules 1964.

It follows that no facilities, such as access by visiting 'ministers', holding of services, provision of devotional books from public funds, or acceptance of periodicals . . . will be afforded and any inmate who asks for such facilities should be so advised.

Although the movement does not have one authentic style of dress or hair, Governors may find that Rastafarians tend to wear their hair either in plaits interwoven with coconut or other fibres, or in long ringlets. Both styles are known as 'dreadlocks' or 'locks'. In support of a request to be allowed to wear their hair long, an inmate may claim that he belongs to the Ethiopian Orthodox Church. It has been confirmed with the resident priest of that church that long hair is not a requirement, and Governors may, therefore, require hair to be cut off.

The Rastas from South London impressed Ronald. They were determined to survive in prison as Rastas rather than be defined and moulded according to the word of the authorities. Ronald reported that they stirred up the youth in the prison. 'They said we were there not because of crime, but because of colour. But everyone argue with them, they were all saying, "What can you do? If you go argue with the police, they just come and batter you down." Then one youth say, "We are soldiers. This a war!"' (This was the time of the riots on Broadwater Farm in Tottenham, North London and Handsworth, Birmingham.) Through these debates Ronald began to understand the politics of being young and black in the United Kingdom.

On his release, Ronald stayed in close touch with one of the Rastas with whom he used to 'do a twos' in prison. He grew dreadlocks, drew portraits of Haile Selassie, and wrote poems proclaiming 'I & I is the possession of the Most High Jah Selassie I'. He prepared Ital food, wore the Rasta colours of green, red, and yellow, and endured the taunts of 'Hey Rasta!' from 'straight' black youth to whom the religion meant dirtiness, criminality, and clouds of 'ganja' smoke.

But what Ronald appreciated most was the good reggae sound associated with the religion, like the music of Bunny Wailer:

> To be trapped and caught and then taken before judge and jury
> Pleading before men who seem to have no mercy
> Battering down sentence
> Fighting against conviction . . .

Ronald went on to join a black music collective which was funded by the Council. He was among 'idrin', servicing and maintaining electronic equipment. He helped set up a recording studio which became the base for the Rastafarian movement in the Borough. He then left to join one of the scores of independent sound-recording studios operating in the area. During Ronald's time with the music collective, it was raided several times by the police. Each time they came looking for drugs, but found nothing.

For Lincoln Fredericks and his fellow founders of the People's Council, however, it was not Rastafari but Christianity that provided a much-needed source of both moral strength and political inspiration. In 1983 the Group who had emerged from prison were joined by George Lewis, a devout Christian and a Deacon of the Church of God, whose congregants originated mainly from Jamaica. A grammar-school-educated former business manager, Lewis was the first black professional to take a leading role in the People's Council: 'I knew of the area and its problems. But the sort of things the others had been involved in—they had been in prison, got thrown out of school—I hadn't been involved in because of my own beliefs.'

Lewis was not slow to proselytize for those beliefs. He set up a Bible study group and introduced the custom of a collective prayer before an important meeting. After they were Born Again, Lincoln Fredericks and other People's Council members became enthusiastic members of Lewis's congregation. They presented their conversion as a dramatic departure from their former lives, and as a return to the fold of family and community after a long sojourn in the urban wilderness.

Lincoln Fredericks preached to the congregation at the Church of God:

Before coming to God I was out there in the wilderness, and out there in the wilderness I seemed to be ashamed of coming to God. I got embarrassed if people spoke to me about being good. In prison I thought good had gone out of my life for ever. But my parents were dealing with God before the day I was born, and now I can turn around today and feel happy and say, No!, I am not weak because I wanna follow God. I believe that I am strong. Consider those who are out there and are still lost, who find themselves every day in the dark corners, because it is a blind alley they are going down!

At the Church of God the congregation was wholly black; men and women of all ages, as well as young children, were dressed in their Sunday best; there were singing, clapping, and triumphant parades. Services were characterized by an exuberance and gaiety quite different from the muted reserve of the traditional middle-class, Church of England, white Christian congregation. At the heart of the service lay the celebration of the literal message of the New Testament, the promise of deliverance from the pain and hardship of life, through Jesus Christ: 'When the Lord comes your sorrows will be ended.'

Thus the Church of God provided a source of spiritual strength. But there were many within the black religious community who felt that an even more important function of the church was to produce leaders, people capable of influencing the wider society, reducing prejudice and misunderstanding, and presenting positive role models for youth. A prominent Pentacostalist, Pastor Ira Brooks, has stated:

On the question of black leadership, I am prepared to offer myself as a leader as good and as capable as any of my contemporary leaders. And I would say that a black man can be as good as any white leader and even surpass him in certain qualities of leadership, or individual qualities. There has been a tendency to look down on blackness. We now have a very good opportunity to show not only the black community but the world that there are black men and women who are qualified for leadership . . . The church is the most fitting source for providing leaders because of its principles and its moral concern. (A. Jackson 1985: 16)

Pastor Brooks was frank about one obstacle to the emergence of an indigenous black leadership in Britain:

There could be a certain amount of difficulty in persuading the black community to accept black leadership. Some people may have been persuaded to look for leadership only in the white society. But with models and, above all leaders like myself not hesitating in training and encouraging would-be leaders from our own congregation all that will be behind us (ibid.)

In South Borough, the Church was proving to be the source of a new black leadership headed by Lincoln Fredericks. It was also the place where the seemingly unbreakable solidarity of the Christian devotees within the People's Council was forged. But the influence of the black Christian church in Britain was not the only factor in the making of the People's Council. There was also the ideal and example of the great struggle of African Americans in the 1960s to end legalized segregation, and achieve equality in a predominantly white society. In 1981 that struggle for social and political emancipation seemed especially relevant in the United Kingdom. The riots of the summer were widely compared with the explosions that shook the black ghettos of the United States in the 1960s, although the scale of the disorders differed greatly. The riot that erupted in Watts, a suburb of Los Angeles, California, in 1965, left over a thousand injured, thirty-four dead, and damage estimated at $40 million. The scale of the devastation was exceeded by the Los Angeles riots of the spring of 1992. But, whereas the latter uprising took place in a climate of political conservatism and liberal paralysis over 'what to do about the underclass', the Watts riots of 1965 changed the course of the black freedom struggle in the United States. There was disillusionment with the non-violent tactics and integrationist goals of Martin Luther King and the mainstream Civil Rights Movement, and a resurgence of interest in black nationalist and separatist solutions polarized around the figure of Malcolm X. The ideal of black self-help, as once propagated by Booker T. Washington, was also back on the agenda.

The man brought in to rebuild the Watts neighbourhood was a charismatic labour organizer and former construction worker, Ted Watkins. Backed with money and resources from his Union, Watkins founded the Watts Labour Community Action Committee (WLCAC), message: Construction not Destruction. WLCAC harnessed the community into a massive programme of self-help. Shopping centres, hospitals, garages, and homes were built for blacks by blacks. Ted Watkins has stated:

One of the real answers is getting the people of the ghetto involved in work and doing something about the way they live, their environment, doing something about the houses they live in and building those houses, doing something about the business that is in the community and owning some of the businesses, and seeing to it that those businesses are protected from crime because they have a share in owning them.

In 1981 Ted Watkins was invited by the London-based Community Service Volunteers (CSV) to report on the riot-torn inner cities of Britain. He reported:

On my first visit to London I went on a tour of Brixton, Haringey, Brent and Hackney. I visited some youths who were based in a community room playing snooker. I asked them if I could talk to them about some of the things that we were doing in Watts with youth. They agreed to let me talk to them. When I finished talking and giving a slide presentation, they give me a standing ovation and began to hug me and kiss me on the cheek, and that night when I got in at 8 o'clock, there were these youths in the lobby of the hotel waiting for me. And we started to discuss how to go about setting up youth employment opportunities, youth training initiatives, and youth beginning to become masters of their own destiny. And since that time I have made frequent visits to them.

Some People's Council members saw their work in the context of a global struggle for the emancipation of black people. In 1985 one of the great heroes of that struggle, and later US Presidential contender, the Revd Jesse Jackson, was invited to preach in the Methodist church. In his sermon to over four hundred people, Jesse Jackson pointed out that, although black people constituted 18 per cent of London's population, there were only three hundred blacks in the 26,000-strong Metropolitan Police. Jackson told his audience: 'We want political reciprocity, not generosity. We want our share, not welfare. We want parity, not charity.' Warming to his theme, Jackson preached the Gospel of self-help and self-reliance, not self-pity. 'Have self-respect. Believe in your own abilities,' he urged. His message to would-be community leaders was: 'If you run, you may lose. But if you don't run, you are guaranteed to lose.'

Like so many foreign visitors to Britain, Jackson pondered on a country where lords and ladies, queens and princes and princesses are adored by the populace. And yet there are no blacks on guard at Buckingham Palace. He told his audience: 'Lady Di may have Royal blood. Prince Charles may have Royal blood. But you *all* have royal blood. You must expect royal respect. We are all God's children.'

But not all of the People's Council embraced the ideology of black, Christian self-help with its tacit acceptance of white authority. During the 1980s, while Jesse Jackson gained support across the United States in his bid to become the Democrat Party's candidate for the Presidency, among young black males in the inner cities Louis Farrakhan became the public figure most admired. To many

young blacks, Minister Farrakhan, the leader of the black separatist
Nation of Islam movement, was 'a more commanding presence than
Jesse Jackson, who is a star to their mothers' generation and still
speaks of inclusion when all they can feel is an alienation so deep
they think it's a place to live' (Kempton 1991: 61).

In his speeches and writings Farrakhan claims that whites have a
plan first to subjugate and then to exterminate blacks, beginning
with young black males, who, he claims, are being deliberately
made the objects of fear and hatred. People's Council founder
member Leon Reed was impressed by the message of Farrakhan.

On a visit to the BBC Television Centre to discuss the making of
a film about the Borough, Leon Reed ostentatiously greeted black
people in the building with 'Yo, Brother!' He (correctly) pointed out
that 'the only black people I have seen in this place are serving the
food, cleaning the floors, or washing the windows.' He refused to
take part in the film, on the grounds that the BBC was biased against
black people, and, beside that, black people should refrain from
washing their dirty linen in public. The rest of the People's Council,
on the other hand, willingly co-operated in the making of the film.
The seed of division within the Group had begun about the tactics to
be employed in confronting a white-dominated society.

8
Confrontation

A T the end of 1981 the People's Council put forward its own plan to the local authority, to move from the confines of its small centre on the Satellite Estate to an enormous disused road haulage depot. This was to be the way forward. The broken asphalt of the parking bays, the shattered brick façade and twisted steel frame of the main hanger—on this derelict site would one day stand a massive business, leisure, and entertainment complex. There would be a shopping mall and space for small businesses, a sports hall, a plush bar, music- and film-production studios, a restaurant, a discothèque, and a live-music venue. Community life would be transformed. Not only locally. 'It will be a credit to the community everywhere,' Leon Reed promised. The whole development would be managed by the People's Council and supported by the local authority. Or so it hoped. From the start it was not an easy alliance.

Watched by a public gallery filled with People's Council supporters, the ruling Labour group voted to back the vision. Afterwards the Chief Executive of the Borough declared: 'The Council has responded positively because they see a community with the same problems as areas which have experienced riots, but responding in a different way.'

With help from the Department of the Environment, the local authority purchased the freehold of the site for £1.8 million, a price which was felt by some to be exorbitant. Afterwards the local authority was reluctant to relinquish its control. It defined the People's Council's role as being 'to develop the project', and offered them only a temporary lease on the site. Lincoln Fredericks stated: 'The Council still wanna decide things. They always wanna fix things. They must've thought we want some Mickey Mouse youth club to play table tennis in. But we said, "No! We, the people, will decide!"'

The People's Council leaders raised their profile. They embarked on a well-publicized fund-raising exercise. They went to Brussels to get help from the European Community. They attracted the attention of the higher echelons of Government. The Home Secretary was among the first of a long line of establishment figures to visit the project. Accompanied by a swirl of reporters and photographers, tie flapping, wisps of hair spiralling in the wind, he raced around the site. Lincoln and his colleagues lobbied and cajoled as he went. On the road outside, a squad of police officers had been detailed to protect the ministerial Rover from curious youngsters. 'I think this is a pretty remarkable and individual project,' the Home Secretary enthused before the television cameras. 'But I don't think you can have them all over the show, because it's very dependent on a particular group of people coming forward and seeing an opportunity.' And off he went.

Despite being labelled a 'five-minute wonder', the visit of the Home Secretary signalled the determination of the Conservative establishment to be seen to be responding positively to attempts by disadvantaged minorities to implement programmes of self-help. How was the People's Council to respond? Reactions varied:

LINCOLN FREDERICKS. If his presence down here helps us get what we want, we will have him down here. But we ain't humbling ourselves.

KAREN ROBERTS. The Centre is what the People's Council worked for, it was to be run by local people for the community. Looking back it was like they, the establishment, were saying, 'How come people like you got this idea?'

Patronage by establishment figures of black and minority organizations is often surrounded by an aura of condescension. Yet, undeniably, a key feature of the development of the project was the fascination this Group of former street youth held for members of the establishment, and this was illustrated by the steadfast support of some of them.

When social worlds collide, good intentions, condescension, and mutual incomprehension converge, with echoes of *Monty Python's Flying Circus*. In March 1985, in an Old Bailey courtroom, a member of the Great and the Good attempted to 'respond positively' to a member of the North London ghetto. On the bench: His Honour

Major Michael Argyle, aged 70: Westminster School and Trinity College, Cambridge; MC 1945; clubs: Carlton, Cavalry, and Guards; a veteran of the *OZ* trial in 1971. In the dock: Everton Samuels, 23, unemployed, bearded, and dreadlocked, convicted of possessing cannabis and an offensive weapon. Judge Argyle addressed Samuels:

I am well acquainted with a number of Rastafarians. I know them socially. They are totally honest and hard-working. They have their own religion, which is fine. They have happy lives.

You are bouncing around aimlessly, getting £30 a week public assistance when you are a trained electronics wiring man. You have to get off your backside and do some work instead of living off the community.

During his lunchbreak Judge Argyle got in touch with a managing director of his acquaintance who ran an electronics company in an outer suburb of the city. The chap agreed to employ Everton. Judge Argyle put the offer to him. 'I know it is a long way from where you live, but if you give it a spin I will defer sentence,' he promised. Everton was unimpressed with the judge's patronage. 'It's too far,' he told eager journalists. 'But if the judge can buy me a car tomorrow, I will start the job.'

The case received a great deal of publicity, particularly in the tabloid Press. The following week in court Judge Argyle looked sternly over his spectacles at Samuels.

I have to tell you that your attitude last week has done your people no good because the court has received a number of letters from anarchists, fascists, and racialists. They were all anonymous, which means that they went straight into the waste-paper bin. But your manner automatically feeds the prejudices of those people who think that any person who happens to be coloured is automatically unfit to be a member of their society . . . You are living in a different world. . . . There are a lot of people on the staff here [the Old Bailey] who have served their country well both in war and peace, who travel a great deal more than eight miles [to get to work] and for wages at less than you could get if you were prepared to work in your trade.

Counter-culturalists of the 1960s once referred to processes whereby the powerful élite absorbs the radical energies of the powerless as exercises in repressive tolerance. The People's Council leaders were natural targets for such absorption techniques. But, like

Everton Samuels, Lincoln Fredericks refused to acquiesce. He instinctively resisted the invitation to become a 'tame black'.

In 1983, with much pomp and ceremony, the mayor of the Borough unveiled Phase One of the project. From the start Phase One was a success. A new crèche was used and run by single-parent families and working mothers from the Estate. Literacy and numeracy classes were started for young people. But in the long run the most successful part of Phase One proved to be the establishment of an Information Technology Centre. Unemployed school-leavers took courses in computing at the Centre, which was housed in the old administrative block of the depot. The I-Tec's founder and first manager, Mark Williams, was a young black graduate in computer sciences. He set up the Centre for a derisory salary compared with what he could have obtained in the job market. Yet he never advertised his sense of moral obligation to pass on his skills to the community. Modest and quietly spoken, he impressed those who came into contact with him with his sense of purpose and his capacity for hard work. He was considered by his colleagues to be an outstanding teacher who could communicate with youth by tapping into their enthusiasm and curiosity about new technology, and thus win their respect. Many saw him as a role model of the young black professional.

After four years of hard work and commitment, Mark Williams resigned from the I-Tec to set up his own business consultancy. Luckily, Williams's replacement proved of equal calibre, and the I-Tec continued to flourish as an independent training and educational establishment. Nevertheless, the departure of Mark Williams illustrates one of the greatest obstacles to inner-city development. As Elijah Anderson has written: 'In pursuit of status and employment, and out of genuine concern for their own survival, the black middle class and those who aspire to it increasingly leave the ghetto behind' (1990: 2). When people such as Mark Williams are lost to the community, the source of moral and social leadership is diminished.

As the project grew, the staff increased. Under pressure from the local authority and other funding agencies to find a more sophisticated approach to its accounting, the People's Council recruited a white professional. There followed the mysterious disappearance of £50,000 from project accounts. Two members of staff were charged with the theft. In their defence, the former staff members claimed that they had planned to invest £50,000 on behalf of the People's Council on the Zurich Commodities market. They expected to make £7,000 profit from the deal, of which they hoped that the People's Council would let them keep half. But the plan went wrong when the holdall containing the cash was stolen at Heathrow Airport before one of them could catch the flight to Zurich. The jury accepted the story. The men were acquitted. The People's Council let it be known that it intended to sue for the return of the money. But years later the £50,000 was still missing.

Following this setback, and with Phase Two of the project—the construction of the community centre—long overdue, the local authority, in an effort to tighten its financial control, introduced a massive cost-cutting exercise. The original architect's plans for an expensive multi-purpose community complex, to be known as The Center, were rejected in favour of a cut-price version. At the same time, to defend themselves against allegations of corruption and mismanagement, People's Council personnel retreated behind a wall of bureaucracy. The Portakabins on the site now housed a finance department, a training department, a business department, a personnel department, a legal department, an arts department . . . There were meetings about meetings, reports about reports. By 1985 the Group's original vision was turning into a paper project.

Meanwhile the split widened within the People's Council between Lincoln Fredericks and Leon Reed. Leon claimed that recent developments had proved that Lincoln had 'gone soft'. He was 'a puppet on the Council's string'. He was 'selling out black people' and so on. Leon formed his own group of allegedly more militant activists, which he named the Panthers. There were echoes of the ill-fated Black Power group which had first appeared on the streets of Oakland, California, in the United States during the 1960s.

There were many clashes of loyalties as a result of the split. Both the Panthers and Lincoln and his Group had attended the same schools. Many were former associates, some were friends and lovers. Some of the Panthers were partners of People's Council members. Others were close to people who worked for the People's Council project. Leon Reed was over six feet tall and of powerful build. A physical fitness fanatic, he set formidable fitness training goals for the Panthers—ten-mile runs, weight training, and martial arts. These sessions sometimes resembled paramilitary exercises.

As an admirer of Louis Farrakhan, Leon was involved with the committee organizing a proposed lecture tour for the Black Muslim leader in the United Kingdom. But Farrakhan was refused entry into Britain by the Home Office, following pressure from the Jewish Board of Deputies, who drew attention to the anti-Semitic content in his writings and speeches. When asked for his reaction, Leon stated that he was not surprised, as 'the Jews control a lot of things in this country'. (When I pointed out that I was Jewish, Leon replied, 'Don't make no difference. It's just that the Jews have got the money and we [black people] ain't.')

There were signs of the growth of a militant separatist creed within the black community. A prominent member of the Support Farrakhan Campaign was Kuba Assegai—his name means 'Spear of Africa'. Assegai achieved national prominence in 1986 by declaring to an audience of sixth-form high-school pupils that there was an 'ethnic bomb' that would kill only black people, a repetition of Farrakhan's oft-stated belief that the white political establishment has genocidal intentions towards blacks. Following this he was banned from all council premises in the Borough. At eighteen stone, 6' 4", wearing 'shades' and traditional African costume, Assegai's image of the rampant black militant was ideal fodder for the racist designs of the tabloid Press. A member of the Labour Party, Assegai used the rare opportunity for a rank-and-file black person to get a public hearing to make a scathing denunciation of his erstwhile comrades. He was quoted as saying that 'only sycophantic blacks are recruited to the Labour party', and that 'the Labour Council doesn't represent the black community'.

Racial tension was also heightened by incidents of black people dying unexpectedly while in police custody (see Institute of Race Relations 1991). In one case, after angry protests at the inquest, some of the deceased's relatives were arrested in the fracas. The widow insisted on going to the station in the police van with her children. Her constituency MP, a Tory, who had taken up the case for the family and had called for a public investigation, insisted that he accompany her. It was widely believed that during the journey to the Police Station, the dead man's son was held face down on the floor of the van by a gang of police officers. The fact that a Member of Parliament was present did not appear to deter them. Shortly afterwards came the death, while in police custody, of a popular resident of the Satellite Estate.

'Curly' was by all accounts a larger-than-life character. He apparently went suddenly berserk one day in his apartment. Police were summoned and he was taken into police custody, where it was later reported that he had died. Rumour swept the Estate that he had choked on his own vomit after being held face down in a police van by several officers on the way to the station. A forty-strong band of demonstrators assembled outside the Police Station where he had supposedly been held. T-Shirts, stickers, and graffiti bearing the legend 'Who Killed Curly?' began to appear around the area. A few weeks later an inquest jury heard evidence that the deceased had taken a record amount of cocaine before his derangement. The inquest verdict was death by non-dependent abuse of drugs and implied a lack of precautionary medical care by the police. The verdict sparked a pitched battle between police and campaigners. Outside the court building, Leon Reed told the Press: 'He never lunged at the police. This was fabricated evidence by the police.' Asked whether he defended the fracas following the inquest, Leon replied, 'I am defending what took place entirely. The police started to grab, assault, strike, and call black people bastards.' As for the assembled hacks from the tabloids, 'You are all racist, aren't you?'

Throughout the Farrakhan affair, the Assegai affair, the controversy over black deaths in police custody and in the aftermath of the riots in Handsworth and at the Broadwater Farm estate in Tottenham in 1985 which culminated in the death of PC Blakelock, Leon took part in public forums debating the issues confronting the black community. He shared platforms with respected community leaders. On one occasion, after a speech from Leon during a meeting, a white social worker and local councillor remarked: 'You want so much to believe in them.'

In the summer of 1985, Lincoln Fredericks found himself fighting a war on two fronts, against the local authority on the one hand, and against Leon and the Panthers on the other. To contain Leon and satisfy his aspirations to power and status in the community, Lincoln arranged for him to have his own domain. The Parade Club on Estate Parade was the main local-authority-funded youth facility on the Satellite Estate. Lincoln backed an application in support of the appointment of Leon as Senior Youth Worker there. There was one problem. Although designated for youth in the evenings, the Parade was used during the day by a variety of tenants' groups, including a pre-school children's nursery and a pensioners' lunch club. The pensioners' club had a predominantly white membership, drawn not from the Estate, but from the low-rise council housing and owner-occupier enclaves in the neighbourhood. Leon Reed argued that the Parade Club's priority should be the unemployed black youth of the neighbourhood who had nowhere to meet during the day. He issued the pensioners' club with an ultimatum to move out. But the pensioners, headed by Mr Ronald Smith, a redoubtable 78-year-old war veteran, refused to budge. Eyewitnesses described how one day Leon and fellow Panthers interrupted a pensioners' social. They put on loud music, set up snooker tables in the lunch-club area, and literally threw lunch-club tables and chairs out of the window. One of the Panthers upset a tray full of tea cups. Another went into the kitchen and overturned the tea urn. Following this incident, Mr Smith had a heart attack and died. His embittered widow carried on the fight. Finally, unable to get the authorities to intervene, Mrs Smith contacted the Press. A series of sensational and often frankly racist stores of helpless white pensioners menaced and bullied by black thugs appeared in the tabloids. A tabloid newspaper also carried a photograph of a smiling Leon and four of his fellow Panthers giving clenched fist and V-for-Victory salutes. Leon received death threats and hate mail thought to come mainly from the National Front. *Bulldog* and other NF and racist literature gave prominence to the story. At least one meeting of NF members, which took place in the saloon bar of a pub situated in a predominantly white middle-class neighbourhood which bordered South Borough, was devoted to a plan to 'retake the Parade for the white race'. To Leon, this sort of response was simply proof of the endemic racism of British society. 'Them's ignorant people, what do you expect? They ain't got the bottle to come down 'ere. Let 'em come!' He pinned the hate mail and the newspaper photograph on to his office wall.

Leon issued a statement on behalf of the Panthers' Committee, parts of which were published in the local Press. It read:

Our objective was to accommodate the youths from the precinct and bring them into the club. Gambling, drugs, illegal activities. These are the usual hostile and malicious statements made against black people in the newspapers which we choose to ignore. What we cannot ignore is a management committee [of the Parade Club] that does not reflect the racial composition of the area which is 80 per cent black. We want the formation of a non-apartheid body to run the club.

Under Leon's control, white visitors to the Parade were discouraged and the Centre got a (deserved) reputation as a no-go area for the police. In line with their community policing approach, officers were instructed to keep a low profile in relation to the Parade, despite persistent rumours that the place was becoming a sanctuary for drug dealers and street robbers. During the day the club's main assembly hall resembled a gloomy cavern filled with groups of sedentary black youth. In the adjoining rooms, older men aged 21–40 would play cards, dominoes, or negotiate among themselves. Late at night, expensive cars containing well-dressed young men would pull up opposite the all-night Petrol Station, lit by garish red neon, and enter the club. In their Burberry overcoats, hand-made Italian shoes, and heavy gold jewellery, and carrying leather attaché cases, they must have been the most expensively dressed youth workers in Britain.

Yet the Parade Club was undoubtedly successful in providing a safe and attractive environment for local youth. This was in stark contrast to the cloistered Portakabinned bureaucracy that was the People's Council project. One Parade Club regular spoke for many when asked about it: 'What's going on up there? I don't even know who runs it now. Why don't they come out and show their faces?'

Buoyed up by the esteem with which he was regarded by the local youth, Leon pressed home his challenge to Lincoln for leadership of the People's Council. When asked why they could not be reconciled 'for the sake of the community', Leon snapped, 'People don't understand the way things go round here. Round here everyone's got their patch. He controls this, you rule that. That way everyone's happy.' This is the gang rhetoric of respect, status, and control applied to community organization. Yet the two worlds are not entirely incompatible. During the 1960s criminal mobs such as the Krays in the East End and the Richardsons in South London frequently involved themselves in charitable work and in causes where they could be seen to be helping their community—supporting the boys' boxing club and providing free Christmas dinners for the elderly at the same time as running protection rackets and allegedly torturing their opponents with electric shocks.

Leon proceeded to mobilize the growing, but disparate, anti-People's Council and anti-Lincoln forces in the area. Prominent among them was Sarah Bell, a working mother of young children, a forceful campaigner for tenants' rights, chairwoman of the Tenants' Association, and an active member of the Labour Party. Sarah protested that the People's Council was undemocratic, concentrating too much power in the hands of Lincoln and his close circle of friends and associates. Yet, like Leon Reed, Sarah was also part of that same friendship network. There were those who assumed that Sarah Bell's vehement opposition to the People's Council leadership had more to do with personalities than politics. This may have been unfair, but, in the politics of tightknit, local communities, it is often impossible to distinguish political from personal motives.

Leon gave notice that he would be moving a motion of no confidence in the People's Council at the Neighbourhood Forum, the most powerful community organization in the neighbourhood. The People's Council was directly answerable to the Neighbourhood Forum, which had mandatory powers over the composition of the People's Council organizing committee. If Leon were to win the debate, then, in theory at least, the organizing committee would be disbanded, Lincoln would be deposed, and fresh elections for control of the People's Council would have to be held.

On a bitterly cold evening in early 1985, over five hundred residents of the South Borough neighbourhood packed the Tenants' Hall on the Satellite Estate. The meeting was chaired by Randall Butterworth, the chief community worker on the Estate, and secretary to the Forum. Outside the Hall, groups of teenagers stood around in excited huddles.

Leon entered the hall flanked by his lieutenants, their leather jackets bulging (so it was later rumoured) with the pistols concealed against their chests. The leaders of the People's Council and the Panthers sat facing each other, separated by a few yards and a nervous Randall Butterworth. A BBC television crew had turned up at the meeting, and, at Leon's insistence, a vote was taken as to whether the proceedings should be filmed. Suspicion and distrust of BBC claims to objectivity in news reporting narrowly won the day. But for Leon the banning of the cameras proved to be a pyrrhic victory. Before the debate, he had exuded massive confidence. He had a deserved reputation as a powerful and eloquent speaker. But his speech to the Forum was long, rambling, and nervous. His allegations of financial corruption and gross mismanagement against the People's Council appeared confused and disjointed. In his reply on behalf of the People's Council, Lincoln Fredericks was modest and self-critical. He blamed the local authority for the shortcomings of the People's Council. He declared: 'If I was up there on the estate, I would see me as another council worker. That's how it goes. You work for the council, they mould you a certain way, you start talking their language, you even come up with their bullshit and start to believe it. But its not real!' Concerning the allegations of corruption he declared forthrightly: 'We've got nothing to hide.'

When, after an exhaustive debate, the Forum broke up prior to a card vote, there was a great deal of private negotiation. People's Council supporters spread word about Leon's alleged criminal involvements. Lincoln later commented: 'Those guys [Leon's supporters] was being torn up, being asked to go against us. They'd known us since we were kids. They knew what we had done for the area. They was being broke in two by Leon. But they just couldn't do it.' Leon's motion of no confidence was defeated. After the meeting, Leon lashed out physically at some of those he suspected had deserted him. The meeting ended in fisticuffs, but Lincoln Fredericks's survival as leader of the People's Council had been ensured.

In October 1985 the foundation stone for the construction of a multi-purpose community enterprise—The Center—was formally laid, although it was not until the following year, after four years of arguing with the local authority, that building work finally commenced. But by then the rift had widened between Lincoln and Leon, and also between the People's Council and the youth of the area it was meant to serve. In the spring of 1986 one of the original sources of inspiration for the People's Council, the US community activist and apostle of black self-help Ted Watkins, returned to South Borough.

He visited the Parade Club and made an emotional appeal to Leon Reed to heal the rift. 'Leon, I love you as a brother. I appeal to you to join with Lincoln, for together you are strong and will overcome any obstacle before you.' But his appeal fell on deaf ears.

Despite initial promises of 'by the people, for the people' there was a noticeable lack of involvement of the youth of the neighbourhood in the actual construction of The Center. Ted Watkins visited the project building site. He reported:

On my visit I was encouraged by some of the things that I saw, but the major thing that I saw I am discouraged by. When I went there, the youth were in the executive positions running their training programmes and running their little canteen and basically running the offices. But this has been an approximately £3 million contract to build the community complex and there was not one black worker working on that site, and I think that is one of the major problems that I see there. In our Watts building programs what we do is bring in a 48-dollars-an-hour carpenter, and we can put a trainee who earns three dollars and fifty cents an hour with that carpenter. That carpenter shows him how to put in the framing and all that stuff. This goes on throughout the project, and what we are preparing them for is the apprenticeship. The way to do it is to mix the unskilled youth with the skilled older worker.

So what of the promise of building jobs for unemployed local youth? An early attempt at fostering a black building co-operative had proved a costly failure. The site was being developed by a major building contractor, which issued a statement regretting that it did not happen to be employing black workers on the site. As one youth put it: 'I'm unemployed right, and I wanna do building work right, and I've been living on the estate, and I haven't heard nothing from them. It's got so a lot of us round here don't pay much interest to it [The Center]. There's not exactly a lot of things down there that I'm really interested in.'

By the winter of 1987 the main bulk of the construction of The Center—'the magnificent dream made flesh' of the People's Council—was finally completed. The complex encompassed space for a four-hundred seat theatre and disco and performance area; small business units—light industrial and office accommodation—which together comprised some five hundred square feet of rentable commercial space; conference and banqueting suites of varying capacities available for hire for weddings and other private functions; a smartly appointed restaurant; a fast-food area and open-plan bar lounge. A central feature of The Center was its comprehensive sports facility. At the heart of the complex stood the Sports Hall, fully equipped to professional basketball tournament standards, with peripheral seating for over eight hundred spectators. Other sports facilities included squash courts and provision for a weight room, an aerobics and dance room, and a physiotherapy service. The modish construction of this multi-purpose complex was in sharp contrast to the converted churches, scout halls, and dilapidated Victorian school buildings that housed the area's myriad community development, training, and advice agencies. But was its up-market design aimed at people on low incomes? Or was it, as critics alleged, to attract 'Bumpys'—black urban middle-class young professionals—like the People's Council executives themselves?

A student living on the Satellite spoke for many residents:

It's a bit far off from us all really. It's just remote, you know. It stands apart from the people. It doesn't stand with them. Sometimes when people in the community reach certain levels to operate certain things, they change, that's it in a nutshell, they change, all their thinking towards themselves, they don't really wanna know the ghetto people no more.

Others continued to criticize the People's Council for being puppets of the Council. A member of the Group that founded the People's Council admitted: 'People always say they [the Council] will never give us the lease. They will always be owning and controlling us.' The Center was once proclaimed as a model of black participation. Was it now to go down as a paper exercise in a Britain where, as far as the black community is concerned, all the decisions appear to be taken in advance and the real power lies elsewhere?

There was also the smouldering ambition of Leon and the Panthers to contend with. But Lincoln remained adamant. There would be no place in The Center for his former comrade. One evening, frustrated and angry at being shut out, Leon walked into the Center, threatened and abused the clientele, and poured beer over the bar staff. On another occasion Lincoln was pursued by a gang wielding knives, and threats were made against his family: 'We're gonna rape your wife.'

In March 1987 the image of the Parade Club as a den of iniquity was reinforced when a post-office van was robbed. Shots were fired at the police and one of the robbers was seen running into the Parade. A force of eighty police officers sealed off the Estate. Police marksmen took up positions around the Parade and a police helicopter circled overhead. A crowd of youths gathered outside the club as the police, armed with a warrant, staged their first-ever search of the club. No one was arrested, and the police withdrew from the precinct. Afterwards Leon Reed, the official club leader who had received the search warrant from the police, stated: 'The situation is still extremely tense. There is extremely deep resentment that, if there was trouble, everyone assumed that the Parade Club has something to do with it.'

Many of Lincoln Fredericks's colleagues urged him to pull the rug from under Leon Reed by engineering his removal from the Parade Club. But Lincoln replied 'Wait! You will see! He is not only cruel to his enemies. He is cruel to those under him. So it will be like it prophecy in the Bible, the ground will open up under the place of evil and will swallow it up and no trace will survive.'

In the summer of 1988 the prophecy appeared to have been fulfilled when Leon Reed was sent to prison for eighteen years for armed robbery. It was alleged at his trial that he had been involved in a series of armed raids on Building Society branches. At the time of his arrest he was still the Senior Youth Worker in charge of the

Parade Youth Club. A powerful personality, with a reputation as an activist, Reed had once been in a position to command considerable support among the youth. But cynics pointed out that, 'for a black man to get rich in the Thatcher era, you had to rob'. The Parade Club had acted, among other things, as a place for the receiving of stolen property. One of Reed's close associates received a lengthy sentence for offences involving cocaine-dealing. Over the years some £300,000 of funds were allocated by the local authority to the Parade for capital expenditure and as salaries for (often non-existent) youth workers. This money was never properly accounted for. There were also rumours that people were beaten up at the Parade. In August 1988, during a 4 a.m. night-time operation, a team of Council workers, accompanied by police officers, moved on to the Estate and sealed up the Parade Club with metal sheets and grilles. For several years its entrance remained covered with corrugated iron. In 1991 the building was gutted by fire.

The Parade Club was not the only youth centre to have been closed down in controversial circumstances. Others have met a similar fate over the years. Some were victims of local-authority cuts. Others were victims of their own success. A mechanism appears to be at work in which the more people a centre attracts, the more it is in danger of being hijacked by robbers and drug dealers, looking for safe havens in which to operate free from the attention of the police.

9
The Drug Trade

B Y the end of the 1980s drug-dealing replaced armed robbery as the main opportunity for neighbourhood youth to obtain large sums of money illegally. Until the drug-dealing scene took off in the mid-1980s, there were few realistic opportunities for youth to get rich through crime. There was little recruitment of youngsters into adult-organized professional crime activities. Jump on a young woman from behind, knock her to the ground, and steal her bracelets; snatch a gold chain from a passing stranger; jostle a confused pensioner trying to board a bus and remove her purse; 'tax' children by demanding they hand over their pocket money or newly purchased trainers; put a brick through a car window and remove the stereo and other valuables: most juvenile crime consisted of such unpredictable, unplanned, ill-organized, often downright stupid acts, which, although intensely anti-social and highly disruptive in their effect on the community, and causing great distress to the victims, offered a very moderate return to the perpetrators. With the expansion of the drug-dealing economy, opportunities emerged for youngsters to make large sums of money quickly.

Yet the importing, distribution, and selling of cannabis and marijuana as well as the powders and pills—heroin, cocaine, LSD, ecstasy, amphetamine sulphates, and various other proscribed stimulants, tranquillizers, and pain-killers have been wrongly depicted as a new menace to British society that threatens to overwhelm the natural ecology of local communities.

In Britain the irregular economy has long been an established fact of working-class life (Hobbs 1989, Foster 1990). Merchandise that falls off the back of mythical lorries is sold over a quiet drink in a pub or café. The establishment of an illicit drug distribution network has not been 'a new and sinister creation set up from outside but an adaptation of long-established trading mechanisms which were already central to the irregular economy' (Parker, Back, and Newcombe 1988: 107).

One form of drug-trading is under the counter, through what were once known in New York City as reefer stores. In Arif's minimart in a run-down section of Old High Road, it is said that drugs are sold along with the canned lager, cigarettes, and confectionery. Arif, a stylishly dressed young man in his early twenties who sports a heavy gold bracelet, manages the shop on behalf of an Asian property company that owns a string of legitimate high-street trading outlets throughout London. Arif's minimart also acts as a popular youth hang-out. Throughout the day, neighbourhood youths, black, white, and Asian, gather to talk and gossip, fool around, or join in a card school in a storeroom at the back of the shop. The clientele for narcotics consists of some of these local youths, and also a passer-by market of people visiting the area for a night out at a club or private party, for whom a six-pack of Red Stripe and some tabs of acid are the essential concomitant to a good night's rave.

Another major outlet for drug-dealing is in pubs and clubs. Not all dealers conform to the stereotype of 'the evil one' with a propensity for reinforcing people's contractual obligations by violent means. Some are reflective individuals, intensely sociable, who are also good talkers.

Short and slightly built, with long hair tied back in a ponytail, Karl 'Speedy' Muller changes little in appearance over the years. Despite his winning smile, he can create an unsavoury impression with those who do not know him (and sometimes with those who do). This is because he 'comes on' to strangers as an 'operator', or, in community parlance, 'a flim-flam man'.

Although as a juvenile he was interviewed by police officers and charged with drug-related offences, he was never subsequently convicted. Speedy talks openly about various scams, petty thefts, and above all dope deals that he has been regularly involved in since the age of 14. The fact that he was never 'done' by the Law has given him a feeling of invulnerability.

Some of it's just about money—my living expenses. Some of it's 'cos I like the people, you know. You go to parties, you get invited to some nice places. Students, designers, advertising people. Some of it's for the 'crack'. Like the rush you get when you go into a fancy restaurant with your mates, and order what you want [with a stolen credit card].

Speedy's favourite trade was discreet deals to young ravers in the form of small plastic bags of 'sensi'. Later he helped supply the 'E-Boys' in the locality. An accompanying speciality was the buying and selling of stolen cheque books and credit cards. Much of this trading took place over a few pints in the pub.

Speedy's business-cum-social life strongly reflects the fact that he grew up in an environment where black people were often in the majority. He picked up street patois and prefers 'brown gal', among whom he is referred to as 'that feisty little white boy'.

Speedy is usually impervious to unflattering or aggressively intended abuse, and seldom gets into fights, although he carries a blade 'for protection naturally'. But one thing that does make him wince is when people comment on his 'posh' background.

After his parents' separation when he was 12, he lived with his mother and younger sister in a 1930s-style semi-detached—bay windows, door chimes, and net curtains in a Crescent of owner-occupiers on the periphery of the Satellite Estate. His father, an engineer, came from Germany. His mother, who is from the north of England, was a primary-school teacher before she married. Although regarded by his teachers as exceptionally bright at school, Speedy was too easily distracted from his studies by his hectic social life, and left school with a couple of elementary exam passes and a higher grade in Art. Relations with his parents deteriorated as he pursued the path of downward social mobility. At the age of 16 Speedy was numbered among the handful of whites who attended all-night 'blues' in vacated apartments on the upper floors of the tower blocks. His parents regretted that their socialist convictions had prevented them from having him educated privately.

In truth, Speedy never enjoyed the material advantages of his relatively privileged background. To earn his pocket money as a schoolboy he had had a paper round. Later he had a Saturday job serving behind the counter in a record store. After leaving school, Speedy received almost no financial assistance from his parents other than his board and lodging. Like so many of his jobless contemporaries, he was obliged to sign on and live on his wits. Like so many of them, too, he took crime in his stride. 'Burglary? Shoplifting? That's normal! It's nothing! Among the kids round here drugs are just accepted.' Speedy shares the view of many US observers about inner-city youth: 'Crime is in the very air they breathe.'

Speedy knows a lot of people. His address book is his most jealously guarded possession. An evening in a crowded pub finds him pulled this way and that in urgent conversation with competing groups of friends and associates. Ideally, a dealer, especially one of the middle classes, needs to be an entertaining, amiable socialite, able to blend well into any milieu, both known and trusted in the ghetto, and smooth enough not to raise too many eyebrows when a delivery interrupts a client's smart dinner party.

Speedy was registered as a student for a while at a Further Education College. He moved away from his family and lived in a squatted house. Then he joined some itinerant friends who were squatting and 'signing on' in Hastings. From there he drifted to Amsterdam (the trip paid for by a lost luggage insurance claim). In the Magic City drugs are sold more or less openly, and the Lowlands Wheat Company sells marijuana plants from a barge moored a few yards from the Police Station. Thousands of homeless and dropped-out youths live together in squatted houses. Speedy admired the uncompromising anti-authoritarian stand of the leaders of the 'krakers': 'They welcome fights with the police!' He blended in easily with the city's large and cosmopolitan squatting community.

In South Borough other dealers work 'on the line', that is, on an open street or car park, or piece of derelict waste ground. This form of trading is often the prerogative of older African–Caribbean men. Dealing, or just hanging out, on the street is an established part of the 'hustler' life-style. If you regard the street as your office, then police attempts to hassle you and move you on will be deeply resented as a 'restraint of trade'. In response, homebeat officer PC Green refers to the hustlers sardonically as 'the boys in the woolly hats'. In the wake of the riots of 1981, Green and his colleagues were instructed 'to show sensitivity and understanding towards minority cultural practices'. He can only watch as Junior, a 28-year-old dreadlocked dealer in Levi 501s, high boots, and a leather-tassled jacket, and with packets of drugs concealed in his underpants, self-consciously removes a wad of £10 notes from his pockets just to buy a pack of cigarettes in a newsagent. Some hustlers, technically unemployed, carry mobile phones and are reputed to walk around the area with hundreds of pounds in their pockets. Unwilling to invest their cash in an Abbey National Building Society High Interest Account, they prefer a more high-risk form of investment, gambling. In a dank room above a seedy café, a card game operates throughout the night. Employees arriving early for work at a nearby factory are often in time to see the players leaving.

There is a ruthless impersonality about the way Junior deals the cards. At a Church of England secondary school in the 1970s he instigated gambling sessions behind the bike sheds. Sometimes he would deliberately lose to the impressionable and the slow-witted. Later, when the position was reversed, he would finger them for favours in lieu of debts. From school he graduated to the betting shops and the Win-a-Prize Amusement Arcade on the Old High Road. Here dull-eyed young men—would-be hustlers in worn leather coats—would gather during the afternoons. Sometimes they would stand posed against the window of the Arcade, virtually without moving, for hours on end, as women laden with small children, grey-coated elderly people, and chirpy schoolkids bustled past them.

In the Win-a-Prize Junior moved among people who had nothing and lived nowhere. They had scarcely attended school, had never worked, were of no fixed address, and were not known to the authorities in any way except as a police statistic. When people incurred debts to him, Junior discovered that collection can be hazardous. Sometimes he preferred to contract an enforcer, a Nigerian ex-boxer, to 'visit' the punter. 'Someone in your way? Well just blow him away!' An enforcer does not come cheap. The money to finance enforcers in the community came from drugs and stolen property.

A young man falls to his death from the eighth floor of a tower block. A school student is blown away by a group of people who knock on his door. Not only beatings but deaths in suspicious circumstances accompany the flurry of drug deals. Superficially, techniques of enforcement at the bottom of the drugs and gambling pyramid resemble the summary justice meted out by the Bolivian bosses of the international drug cartels. Yet it is not the poor, black, and resourceless minority people of the Win-a-Prize Amusement Arcade who have the wealth, the power, and backing in high places to finance the planes and sailing boats, the hefty bribes for border police and customs officials, and all the rest that goes to make a connection. Arif, Speedy, Junior, and their like are the small fry of the drug trade. As Ted Watkins put it: 'In Watts, LA, the cocaine from Latin America came in through powerful big business interests among the Hispanic groups. The black youths on the street are the dupes of the drug scene.' In Britain, the perception on the street is that the hashish and opiates come in from the Asian subcontinent through wealthy big business connections in the Pakistani and other Asian communities, the proceeds being deposited with the notorious Bank of Credit and Commerce International, BCCI, which collapsed in 1991. Descriptions of drug-dealing by neighbourhood youths are often highly coloured by racist ascriptions. Among whites and African–Caribbeans, suppliers of hard drugs are also often assumed to be Asian. In South Borough this was reinforced when, in the summer of 1985, police raided a semi-detached house in a street inhabited by respectable middle-class families of owner-occupiers. The house belonged to a 48-year-old from Pakistan. In the net-curtained living-room, concealed inside the chamois-leather three-piece suite, police discovered twenty-four packets of heroin—1.36 kilos—scales, and 2p pieces which were used as weights. Then, in 1986, another Pakistani, who owned a restaurant in the area, and two other Asians were jailed for heroin smuggling. Eddie, aged 20, is white and a convicted house-breaker. Raised in children's homes, he hangs out with black youths and his proudest boast is that he will try any drug. 'But I don't do heroin because round here that's from the Pakis.' Attacks on Asian shops are often favoured by robbers because of the commonly held belief that they keep their takings, and sometimes drugs, on the premises. Raids on sub-post offices run by Asian people are popular for the same reason. In the Handsworth Riot of 1985, two Asian boys died upstairs above the sub-post office where they worked. The story goes that word had spread among the Handsworth dealers that 'a packet' had arrived through the post from Karachi. When the youths refused to surrender it up, the mob tried to burn them out.

On a sunny afternoon in 1988 Speedy arranges to meet his friend Thompson inside the foyer of the Marcus Garvey Centre off the Old High Road. Thompson, a burly, morose white youth of 19, shambles into sight. He is half an hour late. It is 12.30 p.m. and he has just got out of bed. Thompson claims he is skint as usual. Speedy offers to 'stake' him—as usual—for lunch/breakfast at a café in the Old High Road. Thompson is always hungry. He rubs his hands in expectation. He asks for a fag. On the way to the café they meet up with two more mates. They are white boys in their late teens or early twenties dressed in the punk mode. They are even more bleary-eyed than Thompson. They all sit together in the Restaurant Yiannis, a scruffy café with 1960s Wimpy Bar red-leather upholstered seating. While the others 'bum fags' off each other, Speedy grills Thompson anxiously about a 'fit daughter' he fancies greatly, whose older brother happens to be a close friend of Thompson. The problem is that the older brother has threatened to 'stab up' Speedy if he lays a finger on his sister. Can Thompson put in a word, 'chill the man out'? Thompson cynically advises approaching the girl 'on the secret service'. Other conversations revolve around signing on the dole, and a friend's upcoming appearance in court. They plan to visit a popular night-club for a freestyle jazz band night. But Thompson announces he got himself banned from there the last time, after getting into an argument with a bouncer. 'But they might not recognize me . . .' Two swarthy, well-built gentlemen of the type referred to in police reports as 'of Mediterranean appearance', perhaps in their late thirties and wearing long hair and gold chains, are peering in at the boys through the steamed-up windows of the Restaurant Yiannis. One of them comes up, smiling, to Thompson. All friendly conversation. As he leaves, he speaks Hebrew to his companion. Thompson mentions to Speedy that they are Israeli. Thompson laughs. 'Those guys, that one is Gaby, they were paras in the Israeli army. They've killed people.' They are off their patch— which is the Irgun bar, several parishes away. Thompson knows the place well. He says that Gaby lives nearby and that they have great parties with lots of women, and that the Law cannot nail them even though they know that they are drug dealers.

Thompson reveals that he has been offered a job as a bouncer. He used to box as a junior amateur. His training schedule was an early morning run with weights in his boots, followed by a cold shower. It turns out that it is Gaby who has offered him 'a job around the clubs. I always say no. But he always asks.'

Suppliers like Gaby are

critical actors within the distribution system. In one sense, they function somewhat like jobbers: importers offer them merchandise in wholesale lots; they are responsible for supplying retailers with that merchandise. In another sense, they are like middle managers: they must hire, and supervise the work of several full-time employers, and a number of on-call supporting personnel. (Williams 1989: 10)

A job around the clubs is a supplier's version of a pyramid selling scheme. Suppliers not only look for buyers; they also look for dealers. In many clubs, warehouse parties, and other places of entertainment and work where young people congregate, a kind of concessionary scheme to dealers operates, whereby, for a price, one dealer is allowed in, while the rest are excluded. Often such schemes are operated by the club security personnel—the bouncers. Rival dealers will look to get a foot into the door of these lucrative markets. They will offer to supply or 'turn' a young would-be bouncer such as Thompson, who, despite his physical toughness, is easily controlled, with a certain quantity of drugs, some for his own use, on credit or to be paid for up-front, the rest to be traded at a discount in places where the supplier does not have access to customers.

Each branch of the drug industry involves a complex hierarchical chain of operatives. In *The Cocaine Kids* Terry Williams describes how the cocaine sector works:

Cocaine is a highly valued commodity, especially among the middle class, but because distribution and sale must be clandestine, reaching users on a regular basis presents problems. Thus there are important roles in the network that do not involve selling at all. For instance there are 'runners'— messengers who take cocaine to buyers or let buyers know of a particular dealer. . . . Where the drugs are sold from a fixed location there are 'lookouts' and guards, and often catchers standing by in case a police raid or other emergency means drug stocks must be moved swiftly . . . At the wholesale level, 'transporters' move large amounts across state lines to prearranged locations where a 'babysitter' may keep watch over them.

Import arrangements may involve 'mules' who transport (sometimes unknowingly) quantities into the country. (ibid. 9)

In the African–Caribbean criminal drug networks, young women are often used as 'mules'. In a typical case, two women from the Satellite Estate, in their early twenties, both single parents, were stopped and searched as they passed through the Nothing to Declare channel at Heathrow airport. They were returning from a holiday in Jamaica. Twenty tins labelled Caribbean Fruits and Juices, containing nine kilos of herbal cannabis, were discovered in their luggage.

In the plush, newly upholstered snug bar of the Spread Eagle Pub, a bespectacled, balding, middle-aged, innocuous-looking business man confides to an associate how, unable to secure investment to save his business, and with the bank about to foreclose, he 'took a chance'. He netted £20,000 through importing a consignment of hashish from North Africa concealed in the lining of his BMW. The business man assures his confidant that this was a strictly never-to-be-repeated, therefore virtually undetectable, one-off.

Far from South Borough, in the foothills of the Afghan–Pakistan border, in haciendas deep in the jungle of Bolivia, and high in the mountain fastnesses of Peru, in lands where the sun always shines and where the financial rewards are immeasurable, there lie the highest echelons of the drug industry, the organizational and productive headquarters of a vast complex multinational industry with an annual turnover of millions of dollars. Lorry drivers, students, bogus antique dealers, soldiers, diplomats—all have been recruited to work as mules, lured by the promise of very large sums of money.

For the Jamaican women from the Satellite, their involvement ended in prison. For the business man, this was 'the big one' which facilitated the successful development of a legitimate business. 'That's how it goes. You win some, you lose some.' Lincoln Fredericks had heard stories like these, and turned away. But a part of him would always understand, would always appreciate. A part of him would always be, 'I am someone from the streets.'

10

False Dawn

THE CENTER had been planned and developed under Lincoln Fredericks's often controversial leadership over a period of seven years and at an estimated cost in both public and private charitable funds of £6 million. The development mainly took place in association with the local authority, but considerable financial support had also been forthcoming from a number of other agencies, including the Home Office, the Sports Council, the Manpower Services Commission, the European Social Fund, and numerous private charitable organizations. Despite its chequered history, the project had received considerable assistance from these agencies, most of whom recognized the risks involved, but had continued to back what they saw as a genuinely grass-roots and original initiative.

In 1988 it seemed as though the sponsors' confidence had finally been justified, when the largest and most ambitious black community-managed project in Europe was officially opened by the Prince of Wales, accompanied by the Home Secretary and the Commissioner of Police. They had all been enthusiastic supporters of the project. The Prince of Wales, in his speech to some two-thousand invited guests, described The Center and its founders as a symbol of what a group of enterprising young people from the inner city could do to help themselves and their community. The official opening was a lavish affair. It was hoped that the cost would be recouped through business sponsorship and other pledges of financial support.

Following the official opening, Lincoln Fredericks and his colleagues became sought-after figures in establishment circles. They were invited to lunch at Kensington Palace. They attended lavish receptions designed to promote new enterprise initiatives for the inner cities, where they would be introduced to prominent industrialists and philanthropists. Lincoln refused to be overawed. At one reception, the mostly middle-aged, white, male throng performed a slow-motion ballet around the Royal personage. The subdued mumbling into wine glasses was disturbed by Lincoln's strident tones: 'Hey Charles!' he yelled across the banqueting room. 'If you are serious about the inner cities, we are here. When you gonna come and see us?'

Lincoln was introduced to the head of the Central Policy Unit at Number 10, and the head of the radical right think tank, the Centre for Policy Studies. He had an audience with Mrs Thatcher and had his photograph taken with her. He addressed a conference of police chiefs on crime in the inner city (for which occasion he donned the black leather peaked cap of his youth). Relations were less close with some members of the black caucus of Labour MPs. He was reputed to have had an angry slanging match with one of the more militant among them. Rebuked by the left, he was cultivated by the right. He was introduced to cabinet ministers and received invitations to dinner. Officials from the Home Office dropped round to meet him. The minister responsible for the inner cities invited him to address a meeting at Chequers on Action for the Inner Cities which was attended by the Prime Minister, Margaret Thatcher, and other proponents of the radical right solution to the inner cities. They all applauded his hostility to the left-wing dogmatists among the Labour councillors who held sway on metropolitan local authorities. 'They just want you to toe the line.' They shared his distrust of the power of the trade-union lobby in determining the provision of local-authority resources. (There were no trade unions in The Center, and a union organizer reported that attempts at recruitment following invitations by disgruntled staff to take up a catalogue of grievances were blocked by a hostile management.)

According to Conservative ideologies, the spread of a dependency culture, leading to a black underclass permanently on welfare, was the US ghetto-style prospect for British blacks if they followed left-wing leaders. During the 1980s the number of black Labour supporters who found themselves in agreement with this prognosis grew. Some of them became active members of the Conservative Party. In 1987 a black woman councillor and member of the ruling Labour group in a London borough, changed sides and voted with the Conservatives during a crucial vote. As a result the district was left with a hung council. Her former comrades were furious and demanded an explanation for this unexpected volte-face. She explained that she deeply resented the way that the Labour Party seemed to assume that she would automatically support them because she happened to be black. (In 1991 a former Labour black woman mayor of Hackney joined the Conservative Party, and in Brent two black women councillors, one of them the chair of the African women's organization, defected from the Labour Party and voted with the Conservatives.)

Lincoln and the People's Council, however, always went to great lengths to disclaim any overt party political affiliations. Their apparent adherence to the tenets of the enterprise culture did not prevent them from calling for ever greater levels of financial support from the local authority. But, at a time when it appeared that the political allegiance of minority communities could not simply be taken for granted by any political party, the success or failure of the project was seen by many as a key test in the ideological battle for the inner cities.

The opening of The Center was celebrated as a miracle of determination. The core of the People's Council had held together. They had persevered. One of its founders declared: 'It shows that with God's help you really can get there if you try.' The Prince of Wales was said to regard the project as the flagship of the black community. Following a meeting with Lincoln and other People's Council members, he suggested that the royal charities, such as Business in the Community, might use such a project to demonstrate how the private sector could help the inner cities.

Yet the triumph of the opening of The Center rested on a series of contradictory factors that had yet to be overcome. The proclaimed goal of the project, to become self-financing rather than dependent on governmental assistance, may have been music to the ears of Thatcherite politicians. It overlooked the fact that the project's completion had already cost millions of pounds of public money, and forecasts suggested that it would continue to require considerable levels of public subsidy for some time to come. Another major contradiction concerned the high level of support it claimed to have from local people. At the end of the official opening of The Center, a marble commemorative plaque had been unveiled. On it were inscribed the words of Abraham Lincoln: 'With public sentiment, nothing can fail. Without it, nothing can succeed.' Yet the irony was that the community was far from unified in its support. From the start the project had been dogged by division. Internal feuding, exacerbated by the People's Council leadership's lack of senior managerial experience, had stalled and several times sabotaged real progress. Over the years project workers had been dismissed following acrimonious disagreements over project goals and working methods. After her abrupt departure, one disillusioned administrative worker stated, 'Black people should not treat other black people like that.' She went on to accuse the People's Council management of forgetting its original vision and its promise to serve the community.

Nor was a simple lack of unity the only factor that threatened the very survival of the project. The opening of The Center took place after years of visible deterioration in the quality of life in the area. On the Satellite Estate, travelling people and squatters took over vacant and vandalized apartments. There had been an escalation of criminal activities among the youth. Garages beneath the tower blocks were turned into used and stolen car dumps. Drugs were openly sold 'on the line', a catacomb of concrete alleys. There were incidents of heroin being cut into supplies of soft drugs, and persistent waves of street robberies. Murders and assaults involving the use of firearms were reported. A 15-year-old schoolboy was gunned down at his home when he opened the front door of his flat to five people. A 49-year-old Asian shopkeeper was just about to close his minimarket when he was confronted by two men who demanded he hand over the takings. He refused, and was shot in the face. As he lay bleeding on the floor, he was shot again. A police officer who worked on the case later commented: 'We never did get a result. But all along we felt that a lot of local people knew who did it.'

Outbreaks of public disorder were commonplace. In the spring of 1987, the early closure of a music festival in the Park was followed by an evening of widespread disorder involving several hundred youths. A group of visiting youths from another area attempted to snatch a woman's necklace. In the commotion of inter-area rivalries that followed, a local youth was stabbed. Another young man had just left the festival. He was sitting in the passenger seat of a parked car when a man appeared at the side with a handgun. He fired at point-blank range. His victim suffered severe gunshot wounds to the shoulder. Following this, windows were smashed, cars were damaged, and shops were looted as large gangs of youths spread through the old town centre. Police attempts to intervene were resisted. At one point some three hundred people crammed into a 'late-nite' supermarket. A festival atmosphere prevailed as people helped themselves to goods from the shelves, loaded them on to trolleys, and wheeled them home. Elsewhere mobs of youths up to thirty strong surrounded cars with women drivers who had stopped at traffic lights and tried to force open car doors and snatch handbags and jewellery. Later that evening several other grocery stores and off-licences were pillaged.

Fearing a recurrence of the copycat effect of the summer of 1981, the police pleaded with the Press to play down the extent and severity of the disorder, and newspaper and television reports were relatively muted. But, in an unguarded statement, the Chief Superintendent of Police blamed both the disorders and the general upsurge in street crime on a group of 'a few hundred blacks youths'. He asserted that '99 per cent of crime in the area was committed by black people against whites and Asians.'

This statement, converted into lurid headlines by the tabloid Press, threatened to aggravate the element of racial strife that appeared to underly the crime wave. Such remarks can also amplify the fears and insecurities of respectable residents. After a man had been shot to death outside a 'blues' party on a side street, the police put out the story that there had been a 'Yardie' connection, and alleged that the Yardies, the West Indian version of the Mafia, had secured themselves a number of bases for the sale and manufacture of drugs in the area. In evidence to the Home Affairs Committee (1989) on Drug Trafficking and Related Serious Crime, police officers alleged a Caribbean connection in 'the production and distribution of crack and cocaine in inner city areas where policing is already difficult. . . . This force has also identified links between Jamaican organized criminals, the so-called "Yardies", and drug trafficking.' The report went on:

A dedicated police unit has been researching this phenomenon over a period of 15 months . . . Many of those involved are Jamaican illegal immigrants who have no fixed addresses but who are bound by their Jamaican origin and reggae culture and who travel from one location to another with regularity. Such is their nomadic lifestyle that serious offences, for example murders, have been, and will continue to be, committed wherever the cultural bandwagon happens to stop.

A police allegation about an alleged Yardie involvement in the manufacture and distribution of the cocaine derivative crack from a flat on a housing estate in Deptford, South London, had turned out on close investigation to be groundless. (see Mirza, Pearson, and Phillips 1991; Pearson, Mirza, and Phillips, forthcoming). But the allegation had had its effect. The estate was renamed 'Crack City' by both the tabloid and 'quality' Press. On the Satellite Estate, stories about Yardies strengthened many tenants' determination to pressure the Housing Department for immediate transfer to other areas.

Meanwhile, Lincoln Fredericks and his colleagues on the People's Council visited Washington, DC, at the invitation of a US Congressman. In 1988 they went to Kingston, Jamaica, where they spoke to an audience of twenty thousand people in a sports stadium about their achievement in addressing the problems of alienated young blacks in England, and discussions took place about possible links with a project which planned similar work in Jamaica. In 1989 they attended a prayer breakfast in honour of President Bush. And, while the majority of the people of South Borough remained unaware, disillusioned, or indifferent, Lincoln Fredericks wrote in the project's official brochure:

It moves me greatly to know that the project has got to the stage where local people take a sense of pride in what they have achieved. What we are aiming to do is very ambitious; we are trying to help and encourage people who feel ostracised: ex-offenders, single parents, unemployed persons and many others to develop themselves and re-introduce them to mainstream society on a much firmer footing.

Within six months of being opened, The Center was engulfed in a crisis of catastrophic proportions. The story of the sports programme illustrates the course of events.

Sport was intended to be a central feature of The Center. The neighbourhood is noted for the production of sporting excellence. Olympic athletics medallists, international footballers, test cricketers, and many other outstanding sports personalities have personal links with the neighbourhood. Yet the area has long lacked an adequate sports facility. All the sports personalities mentioned had to move elsewhere in order to receive proper coaching. One of the main long-term aims of The Center was to provide professional sports standard recreational facilities with a view to harnessing new sporting potential.

In the weeks immediately following the official opening, the project announced a comprehensive after-schools sports programme for school-children. Aware that a plethora of regulations—conditions of membership, the booking system, admission charges, etc.—tend to alienate the most marginalized stratum of youth, a local-authority-funded 'Action Sport' team pursued a policy of encouraging open access and informal participation. The 'Action Sport' team's recruitment campaign resulted in over three hundred children a week visiting The Center. Most sessions took place in after-school hours, but those on Saturday morning proved to be particularly popular. The Center sports hall also became the main competitive venue and training base for the basketball club, which consisted of two senior teams, and which drew on a pool of sixty players, nearly all of them from the local community.

Yet, within a few months, the entire sports programme became virtually defunct. The promising after-schools programme folded completely, without explanation. Months later children were still turning up in the hope of attending sessions. The basketball club was in disarray and did not compete for several months. The collapse of the sports programme was just one aspect of the demise of The Centre itself, due to a comprehensive managerial crisis.

The background to the crisis was as follows. Shortly after the official opening, The Center found itself in considerable financial difficulties. This was mainly due to swingeing cuts in local-authority support by the rate-capped Council. Also, a lot of money had been spent on the official opening, and sponsors had still to be found to foot the bill. The Center lacked people with the management experience to deal with the crisis. They took the following fateful decisions. Hire costs for facilities were increased by around 50 per cent. This effectively priced out the community and voluntary groups in the neighbourhood who had looked forward to subsidized use of The Center. But, most controversially, The Center was closed to the community on weekends from Friday night and hired out to private promoters, for a series of supposedly lucrative dances.

Executives from The Center became involved in the promotional plans of a number of reggae stars imported from Jamaica. This meant that in some cases they had to deal with people with criminal connections from the West Indies. A television documentary devoted to the problems of The Center which was broadcast in 1990 alleged that some of The Center's leadership's involvement with these promotions was highly questionable, and at best unwise. In particular, there was the mystery of how dances which could attract several thousand people, and were estimated to have made tens of thousands of pounds in one night for independent promoters, should have eventually proved to have made a loss for The Center, which in any case charged promoters a minimal fee for the hire of the hall.

As private promoters with shady connections, menacing teams of bouncers, drug dealers, and other undesirables were reported to have gained a hold, The Center gained a reputation among locals as a 'den of iniquity'. The personnel of a multinational corporation whose office headquarters overlook The Center ceased to use the place for their lunch-time squash sessions followed by a drink at the bar.

The involvement of criminal elements had a perhaps inevitable outcome, given the course of inner-city pathologies described earlier. Since the departure of Leon Reed and some of his senior lieutenants, all of them sentenced to long terms of imprisonment, the remaining younger Panthers were leaderless and lacking a base. They engaged in a desperate struggle to retain their status and reputation in the eyes of a localized audience. Above all they jealously guarded their unchallenged role as security officers for dances at The Center. But their services were considered to be so exorbitant as to be a form of protection. The People's Council management decided to take a stand. They put the £3,000 contract to provide security personnel out to tender. The Panthers' bid was rejected. For the dance featuring the Jamaican reggae star King Jammie, scheduled to take place on a Saturday evening in September 1989, twelve security personnel were hired from a reputable firm from another area.

Dressed in combat fatigues and accompanied by pitbull and rottweiler dogs, the security outfit crossed the city and entered the territory of the Satellite Estate. Interviewed later on Radio Four's *Bouncers*, one of the security officers recalled, 'I don't really know why I went 'cos I always said to myself never go anywhere where I have to dress up militant. But I suppose he [the manager] wanted us to show these guys that we are not from round there, but we are *prepared* for anything that's gonna be coming to us.'

That evening word went around the neighbourhood that 'raga-muffins' from outside the area had been recruited to take care of security. The Panthers had lost face. Tension was high. Fearing trouble, Lincoln Fredericks broke off a weekend residential manage-ment course and returned to The Centre.

The 1,500 people attending the dance were searched for weapons. But those who were well-known faces were not searched, in order to avoid resentment against a team of bouncers from outside the area; fatally, those not searched included Andy Erskine and Sam Collins, both of whom lived on the Satellite Estate and were, at age 25, two of the youngest members of the Panthers. They were armed with hunting knives.

Unknown to the organizers, one of the Panthers had a history of violent feuds with mobsters from rival areas in night-club settings. A few years previously he had been charged with the attempted murder of two men at a night-club.

Although the atmosphere was tense, eyewitnesses reported that there was no trouble until the dance was winding up shortly before 3 a.m. Then Erskine provoked a row with a member of the security staff who was guarding the night's takings, by trying to remove a crash barrier at the entrance. He was told to use the normal exit. Instead he drew a knife from the waistband of his trousers. Witnesses described it as being like a bayonet and up to ten inches long. Erskine went for the security man, who was unarmed. He was forced to back off as Collins also drew a knife in support of Erskine. When the security man stumbled over a chair and fell, he was attacked and stabbed and slashed repeatedly on the left leg. 'My leg was on fire,' he later recalled. Outside they beat him over the head with a dustbin lid, in just the same way that the Mafia boss Sonny Corleone deals with a rival in the film *The Godfather*. All this happened in front of a crowd of several hundred people.

As the security man clawed his way back towards the main hall, Paul Bernard, who was not connected with any security firm but was living with a woman who had once been the girl-friend of one of the Panthers was standing at the entrance. He was spotted and one of the Panthers shouted, 'I've wanted you for a long time.' Seconds later he was chased, trapped against a wall, and slashed and stabbed by the two Panthers. He suffered horrific wounds to the head, chest, back, and shoulder. The wound which proved fatal was more than four inches deep and penetrated the left lung. He staggered across the main road to a quiet residential crescent, opposite The Center, where he fell dying on the grass verge. When People's Council founder member Anthony Heath arrived on the scene, he was alerted to the fact that a man lay dying nearby by a trail of blood running across the road. A devout Christian, Tony Heath recalls thinking, 'Lord, you are really seeking to test us now.'

Paul Bernard died in the ambulance taking him to hospital. The security officer underwent seven major operations, and received 130 pints of blood, but still lost his left leg below the knee through amputation in hospital.

When police arrived on the scene, they found the main foyer of The Center splattered with blood. A trail of blood ran from one end of the complex to the other. The dance-hall floor was strewn with plastic bags containing marijuana and cannabis resin. The Panthers had disappeared.

When investigating officers attempted to question people about what had happened, they came up against a wall of silence. The word had gone out. Don't talk to the police. One community worker believes that the murderers had acted with impunity before so many witnesses, because 'they knew that people would be terrified by what happened that night. They feared for their lives if they spoke up.' The People's Council leaders, however, immediately issued a statement.

For our part we are fully co-operating with the police to apprehend the killer or killers, for under no circumstances should a man have his life taken away from him in this manner. The Center was built as the culmination of the advancement of black people in this country in general, and in this community in particular, which has taken thirty years to come to fruition. And just as tangible steps have been taken forward, the reckless and reprehensible behaviour of an individual equally threatens to set us back.

To the victims' families, the People's Council stated:

We stand with you in grief, and pray that all those within our community who are right-minded will do the same and come forward and offer their fullest support to the police in their investigation. Let right prevail.

Using a list of car registration numbers jotted down by one of the first police officers to arrive at the scene of the murder, the police tracked down witnesses and discretely collected their statements at secret locations.

A seventy-strong armed police raid on the Satellite Estate was then launched in search of the perpetrators. Erskine and Collins were arrested.

At the magistrates' court committal proceedings, the public gallery was packed as witnesses filed in to make their statements. To intimidate them, hands were drawn across the throat and fingers pointed in the shape of a gun. The detective who had led the police investigation described these witnesses as 'very, very brave'. One of them was Lincoln Fredericks.

At the trial of Erskine and Collins, it emerged that there had been scores of witnesses to both of these murderous assaults. But only a handful were prepared to give evidence in open court, and the did so with extreme reluctance. Such is the fear which the name of the Panthers evokes that witnesses agreed to give evidence only after being promised round-the-clock police protection. Some of them were taken from the court to be given new lives, in new homes, with new identities. As a result of Lincoln Fredericks's and others' testimony, both of the Panthers were imprisoned for life. (A few weeks before the trial, Leon Reed, the imprisoned former Panthers leader, apparently managed to break out of a transit van carrying him from prison. He was recaptured shortly afterwards.)

Studies of violent gangs have shown that a brutal murder becomes the major determining event in a gang's life history. The classic study is of the aftermath of the murder of a 16-year-old polio victim,

Michael Farmer, by members of the New York gang, the Egyptian Kings, in the early 1950s (Yablonsky 1962). The repercussions can lead to the organizational rearrangement of gang life, even to its complete demise. For the people of the locality in which the gang operates, the repercussions are if anything more far-reaching, as residents become subjected to intensified police and media exposure.

In 1990 thirty armed police officers took part in a well-publicized raid on the Satellite Estate code-named Operation Boxer and came across what they believed was a 'crack factory', allegedly one of the first of its kind to be uncovered in the city. There followed at least five other co-ordinated police raids on the estate. The alleged 'Yardie' connection was given great prominence in media reports. Until this time the police had pointed to offences by juveniles as the area's main problem. Now senior police officers appeared on television to compare the scale of organized crime in the area in the 1990s to that initiated by the Kray brothers in the East End of London in the 1960s.

Meanwhile at street level the killing at The Center was absorbed into neighbourhood youth mythology. It became another notch on the yardstick by which the youth measured the relative 'hardness' of their area. The feared Panthers vied for legendary status with the legend of long-legged Yardie Ron, with his white jacket and fedora, £5,000 of gold rope around his neck, pistol, machete, and cordless telephone. As one youth tells it, one night 'he just entered the Academy [a popular dance hall]. He just pulled out his gun and held up all the people inside. Then him and his gang just started robbing.'

Thus the effect of a handful of people's criminality was that the Satellite Estate became a violent gangland and a 'no-go fortress' in the eyes of the police and the media. The dangerous outlaw image valued by some young blacks was reinforced, while at the same time young blacks as a whole were increasingly distrusted by the public and treated with suspicion by the police.

The violence also had another unforeseen consequence. The continued existence of The Center, seven years in the making, and supposedly the pride of the neighbourhood, was being called into question, as news of the murder spread to nervous sponsors.

In 1990, in keeping with Government policy, the Borough Council ordered a comprehensive review of the management and financing of mass estates. In the summer it put forward an ambitious plan for the redevelopment of the Satellite Estate which involved the demolition of some of the existing tower blocks, and a building-renewal programme spearheaded by the private sector.

Under the plan, the web of interconnecting walkways, the lifts, corridors, courtyards, and some six hundred dwellings would eventually be demolished over an area covering half the Estate. The emphasis would be to create as much private space as possible, with more low-rise apartments. The scheme would be an Inner City Partnership. It would be funded by private developers, in association with the Department of the Environment and the local authority. In return for their involvement, the private developers would be given land for private housing.

The Council's Director of Housing stated that the scheme would be the answer to 'the crime, isolation, and despair' which marked the Estate. He went on, 'Most tenants would say that there is nothing wrong with the dwellings, but they complain that they live in constant fear of muggings and assaults.' The initiative would also revitalize the local economy. 'It will tackle high levels of unemployment head-on. It will provide work for businesses and create jobs,' he said.

The plan was greeted enthusiastically by those sections of the media for whom the area's name had become shorthand for crime and disorder. Under the banner headline 'NO-GO FORTRESS TO BE RAZED', the front page of a mass circulation newspaper announced that '£200m. will replace tower estate with family houses'. The article went on:

Britain's most lawless housing complex is to be razed to the ground. . . . Police describe the estate as 'the perfect fortress', a nightmare for law-abiding residents and a no-go area for police and outsiders. Drugs are sold openly, and gangs of stone-throwing youths attack police and strangers who venture into the estate, and then disappear in the maze of concrete walkways, bridges and tunnels. . . . The concrete jungle of high rise flats where last week 3 policemen trying to make a drug arrest were put in hospital by a mob of 50 youths is to be replaced by houses with gardens in a £200 million urban renewal programme to make the estate 'fit for humans to live in'. . . . The [Satellite] was described as the dream estate of the future when it opened 20 years ago—but after it is torn down it will be replaced by houses almost identical to those which were destroyed when it was built.

Patterns of local reaction to urban renewal schemes have been well documented. Janet Foster, for example, records the lack of interest and the scepticism displayed by East Londoners confronted by the Docklands Development Plan in the 1980s and cites Herbert Gans's classic study of people faced with the redevelopment of the old West End area of Boston, Massachusetts in the 1960s: 'people could not really conceive of the possibility that the area would be torn down . . . The idea that the City would . . . turn the land over to a private builder for luxury apartments seemed unbelievable' (Gans 1962: 288–90, cited in Foster 1991).

On the Satellite the idea that rich yuppies would pay good money to live in newly built apartments on the estate was greeted with equal incredulity.

To meet these doubts and criticisms and gain popular support for the plan, the Council organized a full-scale consultation exercise, headed by an enterprising and determined Tenants' Initiative Manager, who organized block-by-block meetings, culminating in a large meeting of more than four hundred tenants. Issues relating to the proposed redevelopment were put before them. One of the groups formed on the Estate after the plans were revealed was the Tenants' Co-operative. This group called on the Council to scrap its current plans to upgrade the Estate and adopt new proposals developed by the residents themselves. The Tenants' Co-op. called instead for the adoption of a People's Plan for the neighbourhood. They stated:

The People's Plan is based on the needs and desires of the tenants themselves, unlike the present plan, which has been drawn up by faceless Council officers meeting in secret with private developers whose only interest is to see how much money they can make. . . . More than 2,000 families already live on the estate . . . under the present plan, hundreds of houses and flats, all of the same design, would be built on every inch of open space . . . If we allow this plan to go ahead there will be even more people squashed onto the estate. What we need is less people living here not more. There should be variety in the design of any new housing. We must make small and friendly communities living in user-friendly streets. New housing schemes should be identified away from the estate for tenants to be moved onto if they so desire. Nearby derelict sites could be purchased and reserved for the plan and used for new housing.

Echoing past community demands, the Tenants' Co-op. stressed how the redevelopment plan would create more work in the area, only 'if local skilled people were allowed to form their own companies and design and build the houses themselves. This way any profits generated by the building works will benefit local people. The money will then be spent in local shops helping to lift the local economy.'

The Tenants' Co-op. also stated that tenants should decide who they want to run their estate, either the local authority, their own housing co-op. or a local housing association.

The People's Plan failed to mention The Center. In 1990 the management of The Center was subjected to trial by television. A documentary programme drew a damaging picture of mismanagement, coupled with suggestions of financial impropriety that must have deterred many potential backers. The People's Council founders were referred to in a derogatory context as one-time street robbers. The programme omitted to mention the low salaries they had received from the Council to carry the entire burden of responsibility for running The Center. The members of the People's Council subsequently stated that they felt that they had been depicted in a grossly unfair way, but that they simply did not have the financial resources to take legal action against the programme-makers.

In spite of the doubts that the programme cast on the probity and competence of Lincoln Fredericks and his colleagues, some of their supporters in the establishment remained loyal, and spoke up for them on the programme. In the TV exposé an auditor testified that, when an embarrassing shortfall was discovered in project funds, a cheque for £20,000 arrived in the post, issued from a Government departmental account, but unaccompanied by any invoice, or letter of explanation.

Following a professional consultant's report, The Center was placed under the management of a white former accountant and professional business manager, who was seconded to the project by the Prince of Wales's charity Business in the Community. Relations with the local authority remained in the balance.

In the summer of 1990 the Council ordered a comprehensive review of The Center and other Council-supported community projects which had survived previous waves of financial cutbacks.

In *Regulating the Poor*, their classic study of federal anti-poverty programmes in the United States, Piven and Cloward argue that Government-funded welfare projects are attempts to foster the political allegiance of ghetto residents, and that, having reached a certain level of development, such programmes are invariably clawed back, as swingeing cuts in financial support are demanded by Government. This is what occurred in South Borough.

By 1991 only the brightly painted mural depicting smiling, united, black and white workers remained of the boarded-up Unemployed Workers Centre. Corrugated iron was the new front for the Local Employment Research Unit, the Black Music Workshop, and the Youth Advisory Service. But not all the closures following the Council's review were made on grounds of financial or political expedience. For example, a local newspaper carried a story headed 'COMMUNITY GROUP SHUTDOWN AFTER GROSS MISMANAGEMENT'.

Allegations of extreme financial and staff mismanagement are contained in a confidential report into a Council funded community group. Last week [a voluntary association] was closed by the Council after the management failed to produce its accounts for an inquiry into the claims. . . . The [association] provides services for the elderly and disabled, including a lunch club. The claims against the group mainly fall against the Principal Officer, and the Chair, his mother, who is currently suspended from her other job as a Housing Needs Officer for the Council . . . It is alleged that £21,775 out of £59,945 of a year's expenditure was met through petty cash. Accounts produced were infrequent, sketchy and superficial . . . Of the staff management it is claimed that [the Chair's] participation in the appointment of her son led to bias against the other candidate . . . staff complain of [the Chair's] 'high handed behaviour, extreme rudeness and provocation' . . . There was no implementation of equal opportunities policies in recruitment . . . Finally the report turns to [a housing project], a subsidiary allegedly set up by [the Principal Officer] and [the Chair] to squat a council house as an unauthorised battered women's refuge. It is claimed over £40,000 of rents were taken by the pair as rent before the Council discovered.

One of the officials under investigation had recently been honoured for services to the elderly and disabled in the community. There were many who wondered whether this was just the tip of an iceberg of corrupt misuse of public funds which had been unwittingly sanctioned by the local authority.

While the Council's review of The Center was taking place, the Inland Revenue was threatening to wind up the project, the gas and electricity boards warned that they were about to cut off supplies, and staff were preparing to remain unpaid before Christmas.

In December 1990 the Council convened a meeting with representatives of the project. The new General Manager made a last-gasp appeal to councillors: 'I hope you will give us a fair hearing. I know the project has had a rather chequered career but we must put all this behind us and look to the positive side. We anticipate that when we brighten up the place we will get a flow of people.'

There was condemnation of the previous management. One councillor, a prominent figure in the Irish community in the Borough, looked directly across the table at Lincoln Fredericks. He explained: 'This project was run by a group of polished amateurs. I recall many occasions of us throwing money at it.' Lincoln replied: 'How can you say that? You have never even been down to see us except for when Prince Charles was there!'

Then he stormed out of the Council chamber.

Eventually the councillors decided to reprieve the project from financial ruin. In a decision that was to provoke controversy in the Borough, they agreed to invest a further £1 million in The Center over the next two years, and in that period to postpone repayment of £220,000 debts owed to the Council. The financial aid, which would be closely monitored, also included a facility for an overdraft of £150,000. After the decision a councillor commented: 'I am delighted at this juncture that we are not cutting it off.' Then, looking directly at Lincoln, he added: 'But I have to say that if you do not deliver there comes a time when we will have to say enough is enough.'

The project's business plan which was presented to the Council stated: 'The aim of the board and every employee is to make us financially self-sufficient. Only by becoming self-sufficient can the original vision which inspired the establishment of The Center be fully attained.' The Council expressed the hope to see The Center self-financing by the mid-1990s.

As the local authority closes down the Youth Service in South Borough, and tightens up its procedures for monitoring community groups, bike-riders in bomber jackets, peaked caps askew, the tongues protruding from their Nikes and Reebok Pumps, weave around the Parade, pulling 'wheelies', staging mock races, and fighting mock battles. Nearby a group of teenage girls laugh, chat, smoke cigarettes, and trade insults with the flying bikers. A young man in his late teens passes by accompanied by the latest male style accoutrement, a Staffordshire bull terrier on a long leather lead. A few months earlier the police, assisted by the RSPCA, broke up a dog-fighting ring organized by a 17-year-old youth from a flat on a nearby estate.

As plans for the privatization and redevelopment of the Satellite Estate are submitted to yet another round of consultation, and as a new business plan for The Center is being circulated, a resident relates how the people of the Estate continue to improvise their own solutions to their problems:

There's a new thing that's come in. They have village beatings there now. When someone in the community gets out of line, or harms the community in some way, they get visited by a group of people—about ten people. Old and young people, even little kids. They batter 'im down. Everybody has to hit 'im, even the little kids put in a kick, so they can say they all done it together. Everybody knows what a village beating is.

As the Council investigates the allegations of gross mismanagement in a community organization and widespread corruption in its own Housing Department, a detective is shot several times at close range by a young man armed with a Colt .32 handgun during a police raid on a house in the area. The police claim that in the course of the raid several kilos of the cocaine derivative 'crack' with an estimated street value of £150,000 was found on the premises.

11
Postscript

T HERE were angry scenes in the Council chamber as the decision to close The Center and place it under new management was taken. Some called it racist and predicted riot and mayhem. Others were less sure. By now the project had cost over £10 million. 'What difference had it made to the area? What difference could any project ever make?', they asked.

Meanwhile, without the help of any community initiative, a new set of heroes and other role models emerges for the next generation.

'I tell the youth, don't do crime! Stay away from trouble! Don't do drugs! Don't go fighting! Nuff bloodshed!'

Marshall Rose is DJ Mikey of Rocket Radio, a pirate station whose studio is a back bedroom somewhere in the Borough. He is a prominent figure among the youth. He is in his mid-twenties, but looks older. He has a fashionable gold front tooth and trouser belt unfastened. A heavy gold chain hangs around his neck. He looks pretty cheerful most of the time.

When he was 18 he studied electronics, but he spent a lot of time at music sessions endlessly rehearsing his repertoire of dub chants. Today he warns 'stay out of trouble'. As a youth he has 'been there'. He first came to the attention of the police following an almighty punch-up on the night of his brother's wedding. Marshall and numerous other members of the Rose clan, in their frilled evening shirts, fought with a gang of Irish building workers who had just spilled out of a nearby pub.

Although he had to go to court and was fined, Marshall described the evening as 'wicked'. A few days later, however, he got into an altercation with the police officer who had arrested him. He was back in court again. A few weeks later he was stopped and searched. He felt like a marked man. Community projects provided a safe haven off the streets and away from the police.

Among the youth, Marshall became a 'super', a 'notch geezer', and not only because of his courageous battles with the police. Marshall was one of a group of music entrepreneurs who set up a string of illegal pirate radio stations broadcasting on the FM waveband. Time Radio, Fresh FM, Traffic, and JBC (the Jamaican Broadcasting Company–these were just some of the black music stations dealing in the kind of sounds that rarely got played on BBC Radio One. Competition between the stations was fierce, sometimes acrimonious. But there was also a common enemy. One evening a detector van carrying Department of Trade inspectors attempting to locate the source of illicit broadcasts was ambushed and 'the DOT snoopers' beaten up.

Marshall is also a 'toaster' or 'MC', a sort of cross between a discotheque DJ and a night-club greeter. The burgeoning live music and club scene where he works regularly attracts thousands of young people to the area. Saturday night dances featuring live reggae bands can attract up to three thousand people. The weekend punters provide a clientele for drug dealers.

Most of the people from this neighbourhood who have become successful through music have moved away. Then, typically, 'they don't want to know the ghetto people no more'. Marshall prefers to stay. He helped look after his 2-year-old daughter while he was at college. Today he is the proud father of two more children by two other women. He may divide his time between three homes, but he is still the traditional patriarch.

He enjoys driving friends around the area in his 'Merc.', the public symbol of his success. He tours his domain to cries of 'Hey Marshall, Irie!' and 'Wha' 'appen!' from passers-by.

MARSHALL. You know. Sometimes I just like to drive round here. This is my manor, my 'ome. I drive past St Francis [the secondary school which he attended], and I look in, and I'm thinking 'Who ranks round there now?'

LLOYD EGGINGTON [nicknamed Eggie, Marshall's buddy]. It's Samuels's brother, that kid.

MARSHALL. Innit? But he don't come from our side! . . . These kids, they don't care what they do. They're growing up now, they don't listen to me, no. They don't listen to 'im [Lloyd].

LLOYD. One's goin' . . . I was at Kooks [a dance venue] and it was ram! The place was ram, guy! The police are saying get off the street [outside].

Then this kid shows me his blade. He's goin': 'I'm gonna "mash up" the police station'. And this kid is like 13, 14.

MARSHALL. It's a funny thing, but when you get to the end of the Road [beyond South Borough], your feeling changes. Then it's all 'danger'. Even Grove is danger.

Sometimes Marshall goes 'down Grove'. The word is that he 'moves' with important people down there, with famous recording artists and their managers. Sometimes he hangs out with the 'hip' white musicians who play sessions in the big commercial sound studios. A little private dealing may take place among this smart clientele. But Marshall won't touch hard drugs, and has contempt for people who do.

Marshall works the clubs and studios at night, so he seldom sees the mornings. Sometimes he spends an afternoon in the betting shop. Sometimes he accompanies his friend Eggie, a former junior boxer, to work out at a boxing gymnasium managed by Eggie's cousin. Black British boxers are among the few British public figures with whom Marshall identifies closely. He is amused by stories of their out-of-the-ring exploits in the tabloid Press. How, after Nigel Benn, 'The Dark Destroyer', won a world title, he walked into expensive shops in Knightsbridge with a suitcase full of money—diamond rings, watches, bracelets, a Porsche, a Bentley, 2 BMWs, . . . and how Lloyd Honeyghan, nicknamed 'the Honeyman', the former world welterweight boxing champion, who was raised in the South London ghetto, had fathered five children by five different women by the age of 25. 'He's just a black guy like us come from the streets. When you're the champion you can mix with everyone, from the street to the higher life,' says Marshall approvingly. The black American fighter Marlon Starling, who took the title from him, had provoked the glittering Honeyghan at their pre-fight press conference with the taunt that he looked 'nigger rich'. Marshall points out, 'He [Honeyghan] is just proud to be a black person who made it. God made him that colour. The man *refused* to fight in South Africa.' Marshall has less time for the cuddly Frank Bruno, with his Savile Row suits and his lovable idiocies, although he recognizes that Bruno, too, is streetwise. 'He is a brother, yes, but he don't wanna know us.' Besides, 'he [Bruno] ain't got no neck'.

Sometimes Marshall has business to take care of. Marshall and Eggie are seated at a table in their favourite bar. A stone-faced young man with a topknot enters. He gives Marshall 'bad looks'. The man barks, 'Hey Marshall!' Marshall replies 'Seen!'

Marshall smiles and laughs, apparently unconcerned. Eventually he gets up and goes over to the man. He attempts to put his arm around the man's shoulder, but he is rebuffed. Sharp words are exchanged. The man leaves abruptly, looking very angry, and uttering threats as he goes.

The bar staff are apprehensive. Marshall seeks to calm things down. 'It's just business,' he explains. 'He don't like it 'cos I speeched him'. Marshall appears untroubled. As long as he has Eggie to back him up, he probably has no reason to be troubled by violent threats.

In his portrait of an inner-city neighbourhood in the United States, Elijah Anderson describes how the relationship between 'old heads' and young men represented an important institution in the community. Traditionally, the 'old head' was a man of stable means who believed in hard work, family life, and the church. Anderson argues that, in the inner city, old heads are being replaced by 'new' old heads, who in some respects are similar to Marshall Rose. Anderson writes:

But, as meaningful employment has become increasingly scarce for young blacks and as crime and drugs have become a way of life for many, the old head is losing his prestige and authority . . . street-smart young boys are concluding that the old head's lessons about life and the work ethic are no longer relevant. . . . A new role model is emerging and competing with the traditional old head for the hearts and minds of young boys. He is young, often the product of the street gang, and at best indifferent to the law and traditional values. This 'new' old head is in many respects the antithesis of the traditional one. . . . he makes ends meet, part time or full time, in the drug trade . . . derides family values and has a 'string' of women. (1990: 3)

In Britain, however, many black youths share the sense that their fathers, having either abandoned the home or condemned their sons' life-style outright, have abdicated from old-head positions. At the same time, Marshall Rose's status as a 'new' old head is not entirely devoid of moral example. For example, Marshall's 'sound' commands the loyalties of an army of vociferous young fans. Other 'sounds' command similar followings. But Marshall is proud that, unlike their equivalents on the soccer terraces, these inter-fan rivalries are invariably peaceful. As reggae/rap artists vie with each other to achieve new heights of self-proclamation, the aim of the fans is to 'speech down' their rivals. Despite the often violent and sexist imagery of rap, its performance is a battle of words not fists, in which women as well as men take part. Marshall Rose is the leader of a 'rhyme posse', not a 'crime posse'.

Marshall also has a reputation in his community as something of an arbitrator in violent disputes, even a Robin Hood figure, a protector of the weak.

Marshall is reclining in the sunshine on a grass embankment overlooking the Satellite. An elderly woman approaches him. She is accompanied by a slightly built, shy-looking youth with an awkward gait. The woman explains to Marshall that the boy, who is partially disabled, has been ordered by some youths to hand over his wages to them when he comes out of work. Marshall tells the boy: 'When you get out, go straight 'ome. When you get 'ome, lock the door. They know where you live. They will come to your 'ouse. When someone comes around, don't answer them.' Marshall promises the woman that he will keep an eye on the situation.

Marshall's authority as a 'new' old head also derives from the fact that he resisted the police when he sensed persecution. The church elders and their supporters in the parent generation, on the other hand, were felt by many youths to have 'passed by on the other side'.

In the 1990s, as traditional modes of deference towards police officers by urban youth have been replaced by more-or-less open defiance, and incidences of unprovoked attacks on police officers have become commonplace, Marshall's previous distrust of and hatred for the police have been replaced by almost benign contempt. A magazine article reported how a group of youths ambushed a rookie black police officer, removed his helmet and boots, and hung them up as trophies. Then, following an attempted arrest of a member of 'the line' for possession, three white police officers were driven from the Estate under a hail of stones and bottles. One police officer was hospitalized and lost an eye. Although publicly disapproving, privately Marshall appreciated such overt shows of resistance to the authority of the police. He reckons that the police are still reaping what they sowed before the riots of 1981. 'For too long they pick on the youth and get away with it. Now they get battered so they don't like it. It gets so the police are shit scared to come around. Someone teach them some heavy manners!'

There are those whose main motivation is to escape from the ghetto. When he was 15, Horace was involved on the periphery of a case of sexual assault on a 14-year-old girl, for which an older youth was sent to prison. He was also nicked for stealing from a newsagents, an offence he admitted, but claimed was a 'one off' which he committed for a dare.

Nicknamed 'Hairy arse' by his detractors, Horace is thin and wiry, with a highlighted 'Afro' and a neatly trimmed Eddie Murphy moustache. Horace was in constant trouble during his time at the Youth Training Workshop, mainly for his 'lip' and his foul-mouthed sexist remarks. He had a mocking, malevolent attitude to those of his fellow trainees whom he judged to be inferior or weaker than himself. On the other hand, he showed great perseverance as regards his skills training. He wanted to better himself, and realized that this could only happen through hard work. He was also trustworthy. After he left the workshop, Horace went on to complete a college course in painting and decorating and become an accredited tradesperson.

He worked for some considerable time as a 'brush' for a big Irish building subcontractor whose operations stretched far afield. The main worksite was some considerable distance from his home, and he was expected to be on site by 7 a.m. He was usually the only black employee, and often had to put up with racist abuse. As his employer had refused to allow him day release for his college course, he had to attend evening classes, quite a sacrifice for a young man with a hectic social life. From this tough initiation into the toughest of trades, he went on to work for a Nigerian-owned construction outfit based on the other side of the city.

Now he is in business for himself. He shares a van and other equipment with a couple of partners. They work mainly as decorators and specialist finishers, but they also include 'laying patios, things like that', to meet the requirements of their customers, who come mainly from the prosperous suburbs that ring the metropolis. Despite the continuation of the major recession in the building trade,

Horace reports that he is 'doing all right', and at age 24 he looks and sounds like a positive advertisement for the Enterprise Culture and its Inner Cities Initiatives of the 1980s. He is married, to the same white girl with whom he was attempting to find a flat when he was a trainee. They are expecting their first child.

Horace's pleasant mood noticeably diminishes whenever there is mention of his former mates, with whom he used to roam the streets. His best friend was Clyde Callender, known as Sweet C. 'Best friend? Why he go round saying that I'm his best friend? I don't move with those people no more man. Where did he get this best friend ting? . . . I seen that Keith. The one we used to call Honeymonster.' This former mate asked him about a job. 'I told him lick my dick first.'

What of the 'badness' of his teenage years? 'You grow out of it. It was all stupidness really when you look back on it.' Recently he had to deal with the police—to enlist their protection against a bullying and noisy neighbour on his estate. He had taken this action with reluctance. He suspected the man was a 'heavy criminal' who may try to seek revenge. 'What can you do against people like that? These days I just try and stay away from those kinds of people.'

12

Conclusion

THIS story of the rise and fall of a community organization against a background of crime and delinquency took place in the 1980s, a decade when the effect of austere Government economic policies was to exacerbate poverty and unemployment and help create the conditions for a generation hooked on criminality. There was a 25 per cent increase in the prison population and a massive expansion in youth training and temporary employment programmes. A host of gimmicky wealth creation schemes were launched at a succession of glitzy press conferences, and appeals were made to the hidden business potential of people struggling to survive in run-down urban areas. Enterprise initiatives were hyped up and oversold to funding agencies. Rhetoric evaded reality. Expectations were inflated. But local people remained sceptical. Some suspected the motive behind all the schemes. 'Black people are being set up to fail . . .'

The end of the decade saw a wave of renewed cuts in Government grants to local authorities. Community building projects, youth clubs, skill centres, and training programmes were abandoned. The Centers became empty shells of little use to anyone, except as focuses for the destructive frustration of urban youth.

Yet this is not only a story for the 1980s. A recurrent message is that a programme for the inner cities, however well planned and resourced, cannot afford to ignore or play down the difficulties caused by the nihilistic attitudes of urban male youths who are involved in crime. Community projects based on utopian solutions, however well staffed and well funded, can be no more than window dressing to camouflage this seemingly intractable problem. As the sociologist Frederick Thrasher pointed out as long ago as 1927, in his pioneering study of crime and delinquency in Chicago: 'The common assumption that the problem of boy delinquency will be solved by the multiplication of playgrounds and social centres in gang areas is entirely erroneous. The physical layout of gangland provides a realm of adventure with which no playground can compete' (1927: 494).

'COMMUNITY CENTRE BURNT DOWN'—this newspaper headline signals the last act in the inner-city drama; several community centres were razed to the ground during the wave of riots that swept Britain in the late summer of 1991. But a year previously another example of the deeper process I have tried to describe—the cycle of youth disorder, followed by inept or ineffective societal response, followed by more disorder—had hit the headlines. In October 1990 the French high-rise suburb of Vaulx-en-Velin, in Lyons, which has a predominantly immigrant population, was engulfed in a week of bloody clashes between police and local youths, during which new community facilities were set on fire and destroyed. The spark that set off the disturbances was the provocative action of the police. There were allegations that as many as two-thirds of them were Le Penists, supporters of Jean-Marie Le Pen and his extreme right-wing *Front national*. And yet the conflict came after nearly ten years of efforts by the Communist Council to reduce tensions. A 'peace corps' of youth and community and other social workers had been established and their numbers gradually increased. Three million pounds had been spent on renovating flats. New libraries and other community facilities had been built. Immediately before the disturbances, a brand new sports centre, including a gymnasium and a swimming pool, had been opened in a euphoric mood of self-congratulation similar to that which marked the opening of The Center described in this book. A climbing wall, inaugurated a few days before the riots, had been seen as the culmination of a successful programme based on the idea of providing constructive leisure pursuits for young people with time on their hands. Vaulx was hailed, not only in France but throughout the European Community, as a symbol of successful local-authority management in the face of racism, crime, and unemployment. During the rioting, community facilities became a key source of confrontation. According to the *Guardian* of 10 October 1990, at the height of the disturbances, seven hundred riot police had to be deployed to protect the sports centre (see also Robins 1990).

Another poignant example of this destructive cycle occurred recently in the United States. Earlier in this book I referred to Ted

Watkins, known as the man who rebuilt Watts, Los Angeles, following the riot of the 1960s. I described how Watkins' organization, WLCAC, had inspired community self-help projects in England. In April 1992, following widespread anger over the Rodney King Affair—the acquittal of some white police officers who had been caught on film systematically beating up a black suspect—Los Angeles experienced another major riot. In the course of the uprising groups of angry and uncompromising youths burnt down the WLCAC shopping mall and other products of twenty years of community development. There were signs saying 'Black owned. Do not burn'. Project workers had tried personally to remonstrate with the insurgents. But these young people were reportedly 'too far gone', too alienated to be reached by community workers.

In fact the riots in Vaulx, in Britain in 1991, and in Los Angeles and the inner cities of the United States in 1992 are symptoms of a more protracted form of guerrilla warfare. In *Slow Motion Riot*, Peter Blauner's documentary novel about crime in New York City, a corrupt former City Councillor and 1960s radical reflects on the change:

'See, people only riot when they want the attention of the institutions,' he told her, 'because they think that's how things get changed. But most people in the ghettos here don't believe in the institutions anymore.'

'So you think it won't be as bad this time?' Jessica asked.

'No, I think it'll be much worse,' he said. 'With the riots everybody got angry all at once and got it over with. Now things get broken a little bit at a time. Instead of one big riot, people are angry all the time.' (1991: 265)

As Blauner's novel reveals, one reason why people 'don't believe in the institutions anymore' is because of the cynicism and corruption of their leaders and their overpromises of better tomorrows. In Britain, inner-city young people, alienated from the political, economic, legal, and even leisure institutions, are structured into positions of wildness and criminality. The refrain of a popular dance song runs:

> The youth are turning to crime . . .
> We'd like to ask our leaders
> What do they have in mind?

But there is little sign that inner-city youth today wish to follow the example of 'Lincoln Fredericks' and 'the Group from the Satellite', and involve themselves with local government.

Is there an as yet undiscovered blueprint for inner-city regeneration which can harness the energies of young people? Or would existing programmes work better if more cash was made available over a longer period? Some believe that the best way to combat crime and drug abuse among the young is not through costly programmes, but through countless efforts of individual will, what US President George Bush once described, with characteristic sentiment, as 'a thousand points of light'. Then there are those, not all of them cynics, who have concluded that nothing works, and that all of the failed attempts at constructive solutions—from self-help to group therapy and job-training schemes—have proved that youths who are heavily involved in crime are too intent on ruining their futures, too hopelessly misdirected, to be reached. Attempts to engineer their emancipation socially simply run up against the basic fact of human perversity. Programmes that run counter to human nature, this argument runs, can even make things worse.

In response, I offer a series of hopeful anecdotes. Once I overheard a young man who is currently serving a long prison sentence for armed robbery earnestly asking a community worker about pension plans. 'After all,' he explained, 'you gotta think about what's gonna happen to you when you get old.' Even those who are hooked on the dream of 'the big one', 'the perfect crime', and all that baloney, may find value in the old virtues of sobriety, self-restraint, and prudence when it comes to money. What honestly is the alternative? Getting acquainted with prison officers? At any rate, 'A lotta shit'.

On another occasion I escorted a group of 17-year-olds—all of whom could have been categorized as 'hardened young offenders'—to a festival of African music held in a beautiful park full of wildlife and flowers. Shortly after our arrival, I managed to lose them in the throng. I worried what they might get up to unsupervised. The next day they were overheard telling their mates about this beautiful place they had visited, with its animals, flowers, and music festival, and how much they had enjoyed the sight of the peacocks strutting in the sun. If you expect the worst from people you can be disappointed.

Jerry Williams, 17, was constantly in trouble with the law. A feeling of personal invulnerability—construed by others as arrogance—and a misplaced sense of self-regard brought him into conflict with authority. The last words from his headmaster were, 'If you set foot in this school again I will call the police.' But these damaging confrontations failed to blunt a kind of incurable over-optimism about the good times that were just around the corner. The trouble was that the only way to get there seemed to be by 'doing crime, going robbing and all this.' He admits that when he was young he had an 'attitude problem'. Today he runs an electrical repair business. He complains that nowadays, in the place of the Law, 'it's the taxman come round my house'. The way he explains his apparent transformation is that one day he decided to make something of himself instead of becoming a crime statistic. Of course he may not succeed. But in the meantime work rather than crime has become the main structure in his life.

None of these moments of hope owes much to extravagant-sounding blueprints for inner-city revival. People generally do not aspire to be guinea pigs in social experiments. Neither do they relish their children being labelled 'yobs' and 'hooligans' by indifferent right-wing politicians. At the same time, active involvement in community politics is too often a case of The Godfather meets Alice in Wonderland. At the risk of sounding hackneyed, what is needed is less rhetoric about regeneration—schemes, projects, programmes, initiatives, challenges, ventures—and more practical help from Government, on a large scale and over a sustained period of time, to achieve modest, incremental gains such as improving the quality of child care and educational attainment, and raising the incentives for young people to work, or train for jobs, or set up in business on their own. This means putting less faith in prisons, which have little effect on crime, and more faith in health, education, training, and child care, which may have an effect, and ensuring firm but fair policing, so that police officers are respected rather than feared or despised, and neighbourhoods are safe places for everyone to live in. In other words, real grounds for hope, not more tarnished visions.

Glossary

backshot: anal intercourse
bail: get out, leave
batter: beat up
blow away: shoot dead
blue: £5 note
blues: an all-night party
brown gal: black woman
brush: house-painter (building trade)
bull: police officer
bum fags: cadge cigarettes
chill out: calm down, cool out
chip: leave
chop: gold
crack: thrill, excitement
crack: cocaine base, a drug
crocs: shoes made of crocodile skin
daughter: a young woman
do a twos: share a cigarette or spliff (marijuana cigarette)
E-Boys: devotees of the drug Ecstasy
feisty: peevish
fit: attractive
flim-flam man: a low-life grafter or hustler (US)
ganja: marijuana (rasta)
grey gal: white woman
guy: term of address, similar to 'man'
hard: powerful, tough
idrin: brethren (rasta)
irie: a greetings word expressing good feelings
krakers: squatters (Dutch)
lame: poor, weak, useless
lip: impertinence
mash up: destroy
massive: tremendous, enormous, powerful
mod: modernist, a follower of the popular youth fashion and music style
 that originated in Britain in the early 1960s
move with: associate with

mule: drug courier

nick: police station, prison

no neck: cannot take a punch (boxing slang)

notch: first rate, excellent

offering out: pimping

posse: a close-knit gang of teenagers and young adults

ragamuffin: ruffian, lout

ragga: a cross between the West Indian reggae and the US rap style of music associated with performers such as Shabba Ranks

ram: full; sexual connotation 'to fuck'

rank: rate highly

rankin': outstanding

roughneck: style of ragga music

rumble: hit, fight

runnings: the rules, the score (as in 'know the running')

secret service: illicit sex

seen: yes, an affirmation

sensi: sensimilla, a type of marijuana

serious: determined, profound

shack up: live together with, on a casual unmarried basis

shades: sunglasses

side: neighbourhood

skint: penniless

soldier: follower in a gang; member of militant resistance in a battle against the police

sound: group of chanters or Jamaican reggae/rap artists, the black British equivalent of a rapping crew

speech: argue

stake: lend money

super: a star, a luminary

suss: suspect

tag: name

tax: rob someone; money obtained as a form of protection

Ted: Teddy-boy, follower of the youth fashion and rock-music style popular among working-class youth in the 1950s, whose clothes were supposed originally to characterize Edward VII's reign

teef: thief

teefin: thieving

toaster: Jamaican cross between a disc jockey and a Master of Ceremonies

tooled up: carrying a weapon

turn: bribe

two-tone: Jamaican ska dance music played in Britain by black and white musicians together in the late 1970s

yard: home

wedge: money

wheelie: a bike stunt, balancing on the back wheel

wicked: superlative

Yardie: a member of the Jamaican Mafia; also traditional life-styles pertaining to the old country

zed: fall asleep

References

Anderson, E. (1990), *Streetwise: Race, Class and Change in an Urban Community* (Chicago: University of Chicago Press).

Blauner, P. (1991), *Slow Motion Riot* (London: Viking).

Bollas, C. (1987), *The Shadow of the Object: Psychoanalysis of the Unthought Known* (London: Free Association Books).

Burney, E. (1990), *Street Crime in Brixton* (London: Centre for Inner City Studies, Goldsmiths' College).

Butcher, H., Collis, P., Glen, A., and Sills, P. (1980), *Community Groups in Action: Case Studies and Analysis* (London: Routledge & Kegan Paul).

Coard, B. (1971), *How the West Indian Child is Made Educationally Subnormal in the British School System* (London: New Beacon Books).

Dench, G. (1986), *Minorities in the Open Society* (London: Routledge & Kegan Paul).

Dodd, D. (1978), 'Police and Thieves on the Streets of Brixton', *New Society*.

Foster, J. (1990), *Villains* (London: Routledge & Kegan Paul).

Foster, J. (1992), 'Living with the Docklands Development: The Community View', *London Journal*, 17: 2.

Gans, H. (1962), *The Urban Villagers* (New York: Free Press).

Hall, P. (1981), (ed.) *The Inner City in Context* (London: Heinemann Educational Books).

Hammersley, M., and Atkinson, P. (1983), *Ethnography: Principles and Practice* (London: Tavistock).

Harrison, P. (1988), *Inside the Inner City: Life under the Cutting Edge* (Harmondsworth: Penguin, 1983).

Hercules, T. (1989), *Labelled a Black Villain* (London: Fourth Estate).

Hewitt, R. (1986), *White Talk Black Talk: Interracial Friendships and Communication amongst Adolescents* (Cambridge: Cambridge University Press).

Hobbs, D. (1989), *Doing the Business* (Oxford: Oxford University Press).

Institute of Race Relations (1991), *Deadly Silence: Black Deaths in Police Custody* (London).

Jackson, A. (1985), *Catching Both Sides of the Wind: Conversations with Five Black Pastors* (London: The British Council of Churches).

Jackson, J. A. (1963), *The Irish in Britain* (London: Routledge & Kegan Paul).

Knight, B., and Hayes, R. (1981), *Self-Help in the Inner City* (London Voluntary Service Council).

Kempton, A. (1991), 'Native Sons', *New York Review of Books* (April).

Lambert, J. R. (1970), *Crime, Police and Race Relations: A Study in Birmingham* (Oxford: Oxford University Press).

Lasch, C. (1985), *The Minimal Self: Psychic Survival in Troubled Times* (London: Pan Books).

Lea, J., and Young, J. (1984), *What is to be Done about Law and Order?* (Harmondsworth: Penguin Books).

McGahey, R. M. (1987), 'Economic Conditions, Neighbourhood Organization and Urban Crime', in A. J. Reiss Jun. and M. Tonry (eds.), *Communities and Crime* (Chicago: University of Chicago Press).

Mailer, N. (1991), 'American Psycho'. *Vanity Fair* (March).

Marlowe, C. (1962), *The Works of Christopher Marlowe*, ed. C. F. T. Brooke (Oxford: Clarendon Press, 1910).

Midgett, D. (1975), 'West Indian Ethnicity in Britain' in H. Safa and B. duToit (eds.), *Migration and Development* (The Hague: Mouton Publishers).

Mirza, H. S., Pearson, G., and Phillips, S. (1991), *Drugs, People and Services in Lewisham: Final Report of the Drug Information Project* (London: Centre for Inner City Studies, Goldsmiths' College).

Moynihan, D. P. (1969), *Maximum Feasible Misunderstanding: Community Action in the War on Poverty* (London: Collier-Macmillan).

Murray, C. (1984), *Losing Ground: American Social Policy, 1950–80* (New York: Basic Books).

National Association for the Care and Resettlement of Offenders (NACRO) (1991), *Black People's Experience of Criminal Justice* (London: NACRO).

Parker, H., Back, K., and Newcombe, R. (1988), *Living with Heroin: The Impact of a Drugs Epidemic on an English Community* (Milton Keynes: Open University Press).

Pearson, G. (1987), *The New Heroin Users* (Oxford: Blackwell).

—— Mirza, H. S., and Phillips, S. (forthcoming), 'Cocaine in Context: Findings from a South London Inner City Drug Survey', in P. T. Bean (ed.), *Cocaine and Crack: Supply and Use* (London: Macmillan).

Pitts, J. (1988), *The Politics of Juvenile Crime* (London: Sage).

Piven, F. F. and Cloward, R. (1971), *Regulating the Poor: The Functions of Public Welfare* (New York: Vintage Books).

Pratt, M. (1980), *Mugging as a Social Problem* (London: Routledge & Kegan Paul).

Pryce, K. (1986), *Endless Pressure: A Study of West Indian Lifestyles in Bristol* (Bristol: Bristol Classical Press, Bristol, 1979).

Rainwater, L. (1970), *Behind Ghetto Walls: Black Families in a Federal Slum* (Chicago: Aldine).

Reiss, A. J. Jun., and Tonry, M. (1987), (eds.), *Communities and Crime* (Chicago: University of Chicago Press).

Rex, J., and Moore, R. (1967), *Race, Community, and Conflict* (Oxford: Oxford University Press).

Robins, D. (1990), *Sport as Prevention: The Use of Sport in Crime Prevention Programmes Aimed at Young People* (Oxford: Centre for Criminological Research, Oxford University).

—— and Cohen, P. (1978), *Knuckle Sandwich: Growing up in the Working-Class City* (Harmondsworth: Penguin Books).

Thrasher, F. M. (1927), *The Gang: A Study of 1,313 Gangs in Chicago* (Chicago: University of Chicago Press).

Watson, J. L. (1977) (ed.), *Between Two Cultures: Migrants and Minorities in Britain* (Oxford: Blackwell).

Williams, T. M. (1989), *The Cocaine Kids: The Inside Story of a Teenage Drug Ring* (Reading, Mass.: Addison-Wesley).

Willmott, P. (1989), *Community Initiatives: Patterns and Prospects* (London: Policy Study Institute).

Wills, G. (1991), review of Nicholas Lemann, *The Promised Land: The Great Black Migration and How it Changed America*, in *New York Review of Books* (March).

Wilson, A. (1978), *Finding a Voice: Asian Women in Britain* (London: Virago).

Wilson, J. Q. (1975), *Thinking about Crime* (New York: Basic Books).

Wilson, W. J. (1987), *The Truly Disadvantaged: The Inner City, the Underclass, and Public Policy* (Chicago: University of Chicago Press).

Winnicott, D. W. (1956), 'The Anti-Social Tendency', repr. in *Collected Papers* (London: Hogarth Press, 1958).

Yablonsky, L. (1962), *The Violent Gang* (London: Macmillan).

Index